ESTHER

A Personal Account
for Women Only

D1641119

ESTHER

A Personal Account
for Women Only

Alice K. Rawlings

XULON PRESS

Xulon Press
2301 Lucien Way #415
Maitland, FL 32751
407.339.4217
www.xulonpress.com

Printed in the United States of America.

Paperback ISBN-13: 978-1-6628-0622-3
eBook ISBN-13: 978-1-6628-0623-0

ESTHER COURSE SYLLABUS

Dear Reader

BEFORE BEGINNING YOUR JOURNEY through my book on Esther, during this pandemic, I would like to make a request from you, the reader. Please inhale and exhale! This Esther will differ in several ways from what you have learned in the past as I have added to her story! As you turn the first page let your mind venture back into the Old Testament time when the Jews were under the power of the Persian government. No Starbucks! No Macy's! No movie theaters! No amusement parks! Although they were not imprisoned they were what we would call today refugees living in the Persian Empire – afraid to make the journey home due to the dangerous robbers on the way. Think now on their life in such a country. As you read please become Hadassah (later named Esther) - first as an orphan girl, taught by her cousin, Mordecai then as the Queen of Persia.

Now to how to interpret her life!

You have been an orphan Jew for many years – raised by Mordecai, a male cousin. Your parents probably died from a plague that haunted the Jewish and Persian population. Mordecai has either been single all his life or also lost his family in one of the plagues. So even at your young age you are responsible for many household duties. Mordecai is a wise scholar whose work takes him to the King's Gate. Your day would go something like this: prayer, small breakfast prior to Mordecai leaving for his day's work and then gardening, cleaning, hauling water, etc. Your excitement comes when Mordecai takes you to market or to the synagogue. You have never had much; you don't desire much; you have a loving cousin; but you are now becoming a Jewish single girl who has reached the age of marriage as we will determine in the book. You dream of this at night. You have probably already dreamed of a certain young Jewish boy but you know Mordecai has to be the one to select your husband!

But your dream has burst! You have been kidnapped by Persian soldiers and are headed for the King's palace! I see you kicking and begging – sweating, crying, terrified just as Mordecai is attempting to free you from this disaster! Life will never be the same. You knew the King was looking for a wife BUT a Jewish one? Never one as young as you! From this time on in the story put yourself in her shoes! Think about her age, her chores, her contentment with Mordecai – then as Hadassah (later Queen Esther)! You are God's chosen vessel to lead your nation!

Make this a book to read as you enjoy the story and then return to it as a workbook! Get some friends together and make it a Bible Study!

Let your mind roll back to your teenage years! Attempt to be an orphan then a queen. Savor every minute of being Queen Esther – a woman for "such a time as this." So from today on be her! Think as if you are just 13 or 14 years old at the beginning – thrown into a "den of jealous young girls" – all who want to be Queen. How do you handle the extreme beauty treatments, the strange food, the eunuch, and your beloved Mordecai gone from your daily life!

Savor the story!

Introduction

WELCOME TO THE 17TH BOOK OF THE Old Testament, Esther. Ever since I was a young teen I've been fascinated and frustrated by this book. Deciding to write this study, however, has been a humbling, refreshing adventure for one my age. A few years ago, when I was in the process of selecting the Fall Bible Studies for our women's ministry, I could not find one that I felt would appeal to women – a study that would make them open their Bible and really study God's Word. Then I thought of Esther. She was the poor little orphaned Jewish girl who was kidnapped and later selected to be the Queen who saved her people. Yes, her story would appeal to most of our women and would fit into our time schedule. I researched the material available on her life, but it all failed to answer the questions I had been pondering all my life – maybe because most were written by men?

Sometimes there's just no way to solve a problem but to get out your own spy glass, your own research books and delve right in. That's what I did. I decided to tear apart the book of Esther piece by piece, dissect it I guess, and come to terms with questions on the life of Esther that had plagued me for so many years.

Esther, in my mind, was the beauty queen of the Bible. I remember when my husband, Scott, and I were engaged that we had two terrible fights prior to our marriage, and they were yelling matches! These were the times when my engagement ring went back and forth from my finger to his pocket like a yoyo. Scott was the youngest of three sons and by the time he attended college his oldest brother had graduated from a large southern university. He had, of course, on weekends filled in his two younger brothers on life on campus. In looking at one of his yearbooks my husband saw pictures of the queens and fraternity sweethearts and when asked about all the beautiful girls, his brother, looking over his shoulder, said, "Oh, *those* girls are the wildest girls on campus. You have to be, to be selected a queen. It's not exactly an honor!" Fight #1 with Scott! We had been engaged perhaps a week when I left for college and in week 3 of my freshman year, I was selected freshmen queen. The truth of the matter is that I never entered the contest but had been entered by the college's freshmen football team! That doesn't sound good either, does it? My job at college was to tutor them (Yes, it was a chore!) I never heard the end of what a reputation I had developed in just 3 weeks from Scott's brothers and of course, my husband to be!

Fight #2 arrived in early spring of my second semester, when, without my knowledge or consent, I was informed via a letter to my mother, that as Freshman Queen, I was also their participant in the state's beauty pageant. (If you know what I look like now you would know much has changed in these past 60 years – it's a real strain on your imagination!)

My husband and I had been engaged for about 9 months after dating for 2 years prior to that. We were scheduled to be married in August. Well, if moms could fly, my mom would have! Had you lived in our area you would have heard a death defying, mountain trembling scream followed by her Kentucky woohoo! That would also have been my mother! I was now totally embarrassed just as I had been when elected

Queen. So, Scott was livid at what his brothers and family would think now!

To add to my predicament my father had just died at age 43 from a heart attack and my family was still suffering severely from the shock. Mom made every coercive move to ask this one last favor of me before I married. I was so torn between pleasing her and pleasing Scott that I sought God's word for my answer – God's answer! Thus, I turned to the book of Esther and began reading, attempting to ascertain if I could truly compete as a Christian. I was mortified when I read Esther for myself! Up to that date I had just remembered the story from Sunday School teachers or from references from the pulpit. Esther was a poor orphan girl who became Queen Esther and saved her people, the Jews, was the theme – or so I thought. I had been led to believe that it was just her natural, God-given beauty that had won the King's heart. Not one person informed me that this beauty contest mandated that she spend a year in preparation in the King's harem and that this culminated by her spending the night with the King prior to her selection!

For years, I continued to struggle with this knowledge. For years Esther lost her feminine Godly appeal to me. Was the crown worth the sin? Does God approve any means to the fulfillment of His purpose and plan? In my heart I knew it was God's plan for Esther, with the help of her cousin, Mordecai, to save the Jews but would He just close His eyes to the "How"? Needless to say, I read and reread but as a 17-year-old I found no answer to my query! At that age you want all the answers in black and white. I had to be honest with myself and realize there was no Godly purpose or plan to the state pageant unless I had missed God's memo.

To complicate matters even further, when I was growing up, the biggest dream a young girl would have was to be Miss America! We planned a pajama party (now called a sleep over), stayed up to watch the annual event, attempted to analyze each contestant, and choose a winner. When the crown was placed on her head and she took her walk down the runway to the tune of "There she goes, Miss America" we'd all bawl! Then we'd go to sleep and dream of such a time as this. Perhaps now it would be when an American young lady bows her head as a gold medal is slipped over her head and the national anthem plays in the background. I remember when our oldest daughter and her friends stayed up all night to watch Princess

Diana's wedding and all her girlfriends just knew some day they'd meet their Prince! To make a long story a little shorter: Mom won. The end was that I walked out of the pageant the third day, and that pageant was not much different from Esther's pageant except the nights could be spent with the judges instead of a King.

So the research that went into this study I pray will enable you to see a book of the Bible that never mentions God's name but a book that reaches women – teaching us, we like Esther, have been born for such a time as this. Perhaps we weren't born to save a nation but even one soul, one changed life could be our purpose. Thank you for sharing this time with me. We will delve into Biblical history, ancient Persian history, God's Word, and see for ourselves Esther's role in God's greater plan. She will speak to each of us and each of us will be her judge.

Esther's Background
Growing Up in God's Word

The Book of Esther (an orphan raised by a male cousin) has haunted me from the time I first taught it as a Bible Study! It was not at all like I thought. How could this happen to a Godly teenager who had been taught scripture nightly by her cousin? Twenty years later and having taught it from 8 different sources I continued to want to find answers! Sometimes there is nothing one can do to solve an issue but dig deeper into the story - learn more about the times and the Jewish life style. Thus I began my search!

Young women then were expected to learn household chores, how to cook, perhaps plant a garden, sell items in the marketplace, be faithful to attend the synagogue, and obey their parents. Mordecai, her cousin, would have trained her more like a son! Nightly he would have shared God's word! As he worked at the King's gate, except for days of worship, she would have played a bigger part at her age in fulfilling the chores of a wife/mother. Once a young girl began her period (per Leviticus 15:19-23) however, things changed. It was then time to look at marriage. At the same time in their lives the King has sent soldiers all over his kingdom to find him a wife. Mordecai would have instantly known this as it would have been interesting talk at the gate where he worked. However I don't believe he thought it would affect him! We see in scripture that Esther knew of him often counting his coins in the evenings and thought he was planning her dowry. She started looking at the young men (only ones she knew he would approve!) so that she would be ready when asked.

Our story now takes its turn for the worst! I truly believe someone in the Jewish community knew about Esther – how pretty she was – and wanted to bargain for a price to point the soldiers to her. Now we enter a new world! We find out about King Xerxes, ex-queens, eunuchs, jealous girls, greedy mothers, Hegai, beauty treatments, Haman, and at the end Artaxerxes! But ladies, whether she is Hadassah or Esther, she remained faithful to God Almighty! We need to do likewise!

WEEK
One

HISTORICAL ACCOUNT

ONCE UPON A TIME (4 CENTURIES BC) King Xerxes I or the Great (Persian name was Khshayarsha; Hebrew was Ahasuerus; and Greek was Xerxes) reigned from India to Cush (located in the upper Nile region). This territory included 20 satraps subdivided into 127 provinces. Xerxes ruled from 486-465 BC. King Xerxes came from a great ACHAEMENID family that included Cyrus the Great, who fulfilled Biblical prophecy by conquering the Babylonia Empire, and Xerxes' father, King Darius, who died in 486 BC according to secular historian,

Herodotus. Darius was to be a friend of the Jews; was called "a chosen vessel of God"; and funded the rebuilding of the temple in Jerusalem. Even Xerxes had allowed the Jews to return to their homes if they so desired. Most didn't however due to the danger/ expense of the journey. 54 years earlier Zerubbabel had led the first group back to Jerusalem and it would be 25 years later before Ezra would lead the next group.

According to Persian history, King Xerxes was a drunkard, a proud one, quite impulsive; a man who disliked detail and trusted few; a man who built a marvelous highway system; and a man who loved battle, conquest, wealth and victory. He had conquered all he desired except for Greece and had great plans to topple it during a time of its known weakness. The Greeks celebrated many days of paying tribute to their idol gods and would not fight on those days. King Xerxes' plan was to attack them on just such a day. When our study begins, he is readying his nobles, warriors, etc. to join him in this battle with a banquet lasting 180 days. Can you imagine the food, wine, entertainment or wardrobe this necessitated? He closed the 180-day banquet, which was attended by invitation only, with a 7-day feast inviting all the citizens of Susa to attend so that they too could be awed by his wealth and power. Susa was the city that housed the citadel (palace) of the king in the winter months. The main palace was located at Persepolis and we'll learn of it later on for its use for one very special occasion. (Please locate Susa on the map reflecting that it is in modern day Iran on the border of Iraq – a very familiar place to us today!)

The time frame for our study begins in 486 BC (over 100 years prior to Alexander the Great) when King Xerxes reign began. Included in the back of your study is a time frame giving you a better idea of the years of King Xerxes reign and of Esther's participation in that reign.

The book of Esther takes place in Persia – which we know today as Iran. Cush was in north east Africa, part of modern Egypt and Sudan. Susa, just one of Xerxes' palaces, was even more elaborate than the one Saddam Hussein lived in at the peak of his rule and would be in Iran today near the Iraqi border. Thus our study begins in Persia, where Jews living in exile, a people without hope, a nation in which most had lost sight of God – heavily influenced by Persian culture, and the setting of our introduction to the girl, Hadassah, who became the woman, Esther – a woman born "for such a time as this."

Before we delve into our book you might find it interesting that Martin Luther was quite an enemy of the book of Esther even being included in the Holy Bible. He said, "It has too many heathen unnatural ties! In fact, he was so hostile that he said, "I would it did not exist, for it Judaizes too much and has in it a great deal of heathenish naughtiness. It is more worthy than all of being excluded from the Canon." He also was against the Maccabees and the Book of James.

Life, as a female at the time of Esther, mirrored much of what you observed in the earlier war days of Iraq and Afghanistan with the exception that modern daughters of the wealthy are allowed to be educated. Passion and pleasure, like freedom, were reserved "for men only". All young ladies grew up knowing their wishes would always be subject to a man's (first their father's and then their husband's). Fathers and husbands had life and death rule over the women. Men, then as now, sought wealth and sexual pleasure. The Persian rule was clear: women were to be objects of passion and respond with children for the estate. The Jewish rule was for daughters to remain virgins, to be taught their female role in the home as wife and mother, and to obey their father and then their husband. Once she was married she would never be allowed to leave the house unescorted and without a veil covering. No one had yet freed their souls. Persian women were raised to give pleasure to the men and Jewish girls to obey and provide children – their blessing from God. Remember the importance of children to Sarah, Rebekah, Hannah, and Rachel! It was true of all other Jewish women. It was the wife's job to produce heirs.

Take a look at the biblical map where I have high-lighted the key area for our study. You will see Susa, the central scene of our book and then going southward you'll see Persepolis, the main palace of the King. Cush is down in the left-hand corner. Compare these pin-pointed areas to the modern map and you can visualize the setting of our study. Susa is situated on the border of Iraq and Iran; with Persepolis clearly in today's Iran. As King Xerxes reigned from Cush to India you can now imagine the size of his kingdom and thus the distance traveled to find him a Queen. You must be able to visualize the great span of races and ethnic groups. Please refer back to these maps when you are studying!

Remember when your mom told you growing up that you never really know someone unless you walk in their shoes. Well, I believe that. The best way you as a woman can understand Esther is to put yourself in her shoes or shall we say sandals. When she's a teen you have to think as a teen taking into consideration her culture – where and how she lived, what she ate, what she did all day, the environment she was living in, -- basically her situation in life. She was orphaned and being raised by a single male cousin. Ladies just think! We get to spend the entire study daydreaming! Let your imaginations run wild. For those of us older we'll get to be young and beautiful! We'll marry the King! We'll save a nation! So, I challenge each of you to really get into the book. God will be working with each of you to get you to understand why Esther was even included in the Bible. Why and what we learn from this marvelous book will differ with each of us. Pray for His intervention into your study. Grab a cup of coffee, tea, or hot chocolate; turn on some soft instrumental praise music; curl up in your favorite chair and let your entire being absorb His Word as you read today. Now read Chapter 1-2:11. Yes, I know this is twice but God's personal message to you will be revealed as you delve into His Word. You, too, were born for such a time as this and may I add in such a place as this.

Lesson One Homework

Please read the entire book of Esther, but this time remember, You are Esther! Answer the following questions in the first person.

1. Note the scripture reference(s) to your parents and describe what you think happened to them – how old you were, etc.:

_____

_____

_____

_____

_____

_____

_____

_____

_____

_____

2. Explain how Mordecai is related to you and why you think he was selected to be your guardian:

_____

_____

_____

_____

_____

_____

_____

_____

_____

_____

_____

_____

_____

_____

3. Describe how you are being raised by Mordecai as you are growing up. Check out the Jewish family customs of raising a daughter:

_____

_____

_____

_____

_____

_____

_____

_____

_____

_____

_____

_____

_____

4. Describe yourself physically (your age, coloring, dress, education, etc.) just prior to being taken against your will to the citadel for the selection of the new queen:

---

5. How did you determine the age you gave yourself in question 4?

_____

_____

_____

_____

_____

_____

_____

_____

_____

_____

_____

_____

_____

_____

6. What is your Hebrew name, its meaning, and why was it changed to Esther? Who changed your name?

_____

_____

_____

_____

_____

_____

_____

_____

_____

_____

_____

_____

_____

_____

_____

_____

7. Why do you think Queen Vashti refused to obey King Xerxes' command?

_____

_____

_____

_____

_____

_____

_____

_____

_____

_____

_____

_____

_____

8. Why did Queen Vashti's disobedience displease King Xerxes and his wise men?

_____

_____

_____

_____

_____

_____

_____

_____

_____

_____

_____

_____

_____

9. As a young Jewish girl, what did you think of the command given by King Xerxes to his entire kingdom that "every man should be ruler over his household?" Was it a new revelation to the Persians? To the Jews? Did you and Mordecai discuss it?

_____

_____

_____

_____

_____

_____

_____

_____

_____

_____

_____

You will see as you think these things over, you take on the mind of a young Jewish girl and can relive her kidnapping and its affect. You'll be writing your own story of this young maiden's development into the woman God created her to become!

WEEK
Two

READ ESTHER
CHAPTER 1 & 2

TURN IN YOUR BIBLES TO OUR CURRENT favorite book, Esther. Basically in chapter one, we are told about the 180 day feast given by King Xerxes concluding with the incident of Queen Vashti being exiled for not obeying the King's command. Let's begin reading at verse one. The word citadel is just another name for palace. The author goes to great length to basically describe the opulence of the palace. White and blue linen were only owned by the wealthiest and the exotic furniture which sounded rather hard to sit on to me was much like the marble seen in the structure of the Taj Mahal. The mosaic pavement must have been gorgeous. Xerxes made a point of each guest having a goblet of their own ~ different from the other guests' goblets and his servants were told to serve all the wine his guests requested. Can you imagine the DUI's – donkeys ridden under the influence! When reading of the individual goblets per guest, I couldn't help but laugh as every time the grandchildren come to visit (there are 16) I use a sharpie to write their names on their red plastic cups and I guess that would be "unique to each".

While the King was giving his banquet it is noted that Queen Vashti also was hosting a banquet. It is not clear if this refers to the 180-day banquet or the 7 day banquet. We do know that it was on the 7th day when King Xerxes commands the Queen's presence and his command is disobeyed which leads us to our first discussion of the day. Queen Vashti at this time was known as the most beautiful woman in the world. It was said that men were left breathless when viewing her. One quote I particularly liked, "She was a woman who commanded the imagination of every man who saw her." He had shown off his physical wealth to everyone and now was going to show off his wife, his Queen. We know some basic facts. One, he was drunk! Two, it was against Persian custom for a Queen to appear at a public gathering. But other than that, we also know to disobey the king brought certain death or exile. Why do you think she disobeyed? (Could stop here for discussion as that was one of your homework questions.) Now for what history says: First, history records Queen Vashti gave birth to the king's heir, Artaxerxes, in that same year (483 BC), Thus Queen Vashti was probably pregnant at the time of the request or had just given birth to the heir. Some say that's the only reason she was not killed on the spot but exiled instead. Being the mother of the heir held her in higher esteem. Secondly, she may have detested the drunkenness, and this had been going on up to 6 months. BUT the most interesting reason given in Persian history and let's read verse 1:11 – is (according to scholars) she was requested to wear ONLY her royal crown! Pregnant or just after giving birth and asked to appear naked would be a little much even for a heathen queen. Then we have Xerxes calling in his special advisors. Remember how the wise men for the pharaohs were always afraid to tell the king bad news?

Well, these 7 were no different. Earlier in the chapter, 7 eunuchs were sent to get the Queen and now 7 wise men (the 7 princes of Persia) his special advisors, are asked what to do about the Queen's refusal to obey. (Why 7 of each? Breaks a tie!) Why were the king's wise men upset? (#8) No one should be allowed to disobey the king! So the wise men, with the king's full permission issued a decree, "every man should be ruler over his own household." DUD! They thought this would quiet the situation but to me it was a perfect example of how men and women think differently. (#7) I would have thought such a decree would have made him the laughingstock of the empire!

(Another example of how men and women think differently – but that's another study.)

Several years pass between Chapter 1 and Chapter 2 of Esther. We will see gaps like this throughout the entire book. According to your Timeline King Xerxes had been in power three years when the book opens. Between 483 and 480 we know that the king had gone off to battle – won one, lost one, and had come home defeated and depressed. As noted on your Timeline he won a great battle at Thermopylae BUT was defeated at a battle at Salamis where he watched half to one third of his navy destroyed. Check out these two sites on the map. This is when we begin Chapter 2. "Later" is much later!

Knowing the King was depressed, his personal attendants (in charge of his welfare; ones mentioned earlier who went to summon the Queen) attempted to cheer him up. How? By proposing a search be made for a new queen – one worthy of the King. Their proposal stated that all the beautiful young virgins, were to be, shall we say, herded up and brought to Susa by the king's appointed commissioners, and placed under the care of Hegai, the king's eunuch. Notice back in Chapter 1:10, Hegai is not one of the 7 personal attendants of the King – no, Hegai is in charge of the King's women, the Harem. They advise the King that he can chose the one who pleases him the best –I will let your imagination figure that one out. This pleased the King and the decree went out. Another item for your thoughts is why did they deviate from the future Queen being of royal blood? This edict to bring in all virgins regardless of their lineage was unheard of at this time. The virgins brought into the harem, often as gifts from other dignitaries, did not have to be of royal blood, but his queen should have.

We are now introduced to our underlying key character - that of Mordecai! Let's examine verses 5-7. We are told about Mordecai who is often erroneously called Hadassah's uncle. We are told about his relationship to Hadassah. Now let's discuss your homework question #1. What do you think happened to your parents? Scripture says "died" not killed – but the word used could be either. My research leads me to believe they weren't killed. When the Jews were taken into captivity her parents would have probably not been born yet. History records that most likely they died of one of the plagues so prevalent at that time. What relationship is Mordecai to you? There was a Mordecai that was carried into exile from Jerusalem by Nebuchadnezzar, but it is not our Mordecai. This man would have to have been over 100 by the time of Esther. It was probably his great grandparents. So who were your parents? (Verse 15) Discuss question #2. Mordecai's uncle, Abihail, was Hadassah's father. He and Mordecai's father would have been brothers. Thus, Hadassah was Mordecai's cousin. As we are not told if Mordecai was or ever had been married, either due to a lack of finances, no living father to arrange his marriage, or perhaps he had been married and his wife had also died in one of the plagues and there were no children. Your guess is as good as mine but decide on one for your imaginary trip into the life of Esther. In your answer to question 3, how do you think a bachelor Jew would have raised a young female cousin? My opinion – he would have raised her exactly according to Jewish law. Having to address the question, "Why did no one seem aware that Esther was a Jew" intrigues me. To visibly discern a Jew from a Gentile today is almost impossible. But in 463 BC the Jewish attire and lifestyle would have set them apart. To add to the query, the Jews were allowed to freely live there or return to Jerusalem. The only logical answer to me is that the Jews that remained faithful to Yahweh never felt safe in a foreign country and thus practiced their faith underground as many Christians did in the early church. According to question #4, how did you describe yourself at the time of the selection? I will let you dwell on that one as we are told in verse 7b that you are lovely in form and features and as our study moves on we find out just how very beautiful you really are, inside and out. How old do you think you were? According to Jewish law a young girl became a woman when her menstrual cycle began. Believe it or not, this news was shared by all. I guess instead of a

Bar Mitzvah which Jewish boys celebrated when they turned 13, they had a Bar Menstrual for the girls. Yes, I'm kidding! Once they could physically become pregnant they were considered to be of marrying age. So how old were you? Looking back on that time in your life were you ready for marriage? I was one of those rare "children" whose cycle began at age 7 so the answer to that question for me is quite easy. I also had a child after each of my two sterilization surgeries so to the Jews I'm certain I would have been a problem! What was your Hebrew name? (verse 7) Why was it changed to Esther? Was it to hide the fact that you were Jewish? Notice change from verse 7 to Esther in verse 8 and answer in verse 10.

As an added note while we're here, I researched a rather famous Jewish lady currently speaking in temples all over the US, and her knowledge of Esther, the book and the person. I have to admit I almost laughed reading her speeches. "Let us look at Esther … her father died while her mother was still pregnant with Esther; her mother dies at her birth. Thus, she came into this world with the gaping wound of belonging to no one. Her Uncle Mordecai who later became her spiritual guide and ultimately her husband, etc. The Maharal of

Prague (16th Century) tells us that the circumstances of her birth were no coincidence. Alienation and loneliness are tools --- given to us to enable us to become who we can be." So the confusion on the book and person of Esther continues to grow even with modern so-called Jewish scholars. I was wondering how Esther passed the "virgin" test if married to Mordecai, she believed Mordecai was Esther's uncle, etc. But - at least she added in the rest of her article the godliness of Esther even if God's name is never mentioned in the book. Few male scholars do this or at least most question it. Some even make fun of those who do.

Now we have another gap in time. Once the decree was given for the selection process to begin several months elapsed for the travel required throughout the entire area. Remember how vast the Persian Empire was. It had to have taken several months for the commissioners to collect the young virgins and return with them to Susa (excluding the ones directly from Susa). The commissioners all knew not to pick any young virgins that would not meet the king's guidelines. Different reference books speak of attempted briberies by certain royals to get their shall we say, "ugly stepdaughters", included in the process. But the commissioners all knew their position was at stake and perhaps even their lives if they did not follow their instructions. Thus women from all over the area were brought in as they were selected. Estimates range in number from over 400 to 1400. There would have been many differences in the array of women from so many nationalities.

We have discussed Queen Vashti, King Xerxes 1, Mordecai and Hadassah/Esther to a degree. According to Herbert Lockyer in "All the Kings and Queens of the Bible", the double name of the queen is worthy of note. Her original Hebrew name was Hadassah, meaning a 'myrtle' possibly because from her infancy she was distinguished for her loveliness of form and countenance. The myrtle was a plant of sweet-scented and luxuriant beauty. Esther became her Persian name when she was chosen as Queen. This name has the meaning of the similar Greek word, Aster, meaning a "star". Lockyer also says "Rabbi Yehudah derives "Esther" from "sathes", meaning "to hide", because she was hidden in her guardian's house, and her nationality also was concealed until she felt it opportune to reveal it."

Now to her beauty. How would the commissioners have known about Hadassah's beauty to have directed their soldiers to kidnap her? My thoughts are that in

Mordecai's curriculum for raising Hadassah he would have perhaps raised her more like a son. There was only the two of them. He had to be lonely at nights and as a well-known Jew he read his scrolls, prayed at all the appropriate times, and Hadassah would have been taught the law. Look back for a moment to Leviticus 12. There are rules covering everything from mildew to infectious sores to bald heads. Someone would have to have taught Esther the Jewish laws, especially, of purification. Here is where a female family member would have come in handy. I am led to think that Mordecai would have chosen an older Jewish woman to teach her. She would have had all this knowledge by the time she became a woman in the Jewish tradition. Back to her beauty. Most historians believe that Hadassah, not unlike other Jewish girls, sold either something she baked, sewed, or raised at the village marketplace to earn money. The marketplaces were filled with Persian soldiers and as was their reputation, they were always on the lookout for young virgins. Knowing Hadassah was naturally beautiful, I think Mordecai would have hidden that beauty the best he could for humility purposes. I'm almost certain Hadassah would not have dressed well nor would she have been dressed to entice a soldier. One rumor was that a fellow Jew knew of her beauty and sold his knowledge of her to one of the commissioners. History records that many girls were excited about the process and worked for days to prepare to be taken while many parents wished this on their daughters as it would be one less mouth to feed and money was given to the parents of these girls. Thus, they prepared their daughters to be taken even against their wills. Hadassah would not have been made ready to be taken! One scholar, evidently unfamiliar with Mordecai, said that Mordecai wanted her there to be a Jewish spy. When picked up it would have been a dreadful scene of leaving Mordecai and the fear of entering the Persian harem. Can you feel her fear? Can you understand her shock and dismay by other girls being so ready and willing? Can you hear Mordecai whispering in your ear that he'll check on you daily and for you to never let anyone know you're a Jew? You are just an orphaned teen who has already dealt with the death of both parents, is living in exile, and is probably already dreaming of Mordecai's selection of a young Jewish husband. Aren't you terrified? The scene I visualize is one of the Jewish women being taken into captivity by the Germans and the fear pictured on their faces. Many were being snatched away from their husbands or their children. Hadassah would have known one terrible fact. Once you enter the king's harem you never come out! Not high on my list of things I want to do when I grow up!

I'm going to save the character of Haman until later but feel it is imperative for you to know about Hegai. He is key to the king's selection process. Let's re-read Chapter 2:3 towards the end "…Let them be placed under the care of Hegai, the King's eunuch, who is in charge of the women; and let beauty treatments be given to them."

We've run into the term "eunuch" before when we were talking about the king's eunuchs who were sent after Queen Vashti. What exactly is a eunuch? What I'm about to tell you is fact not fiction and rather graphic. When some young boys reached manhood, as determined by their culture, they were sold by their families or sometimes just taken to work in the King's service – not just true in the case of King Xerxes but true throughout Biblical history. The boys were led supposedly to airless, hot homes in the countryside thinking they were going into the King's service and many eagerly went dreaming of a better life away from home. One by one they were led into a room where a man waited with a table of simple things – a knife, some twine and a bottle of an amber honey. The young men were mystified as to why they kept hearing screaming up in front of them until it became their time. They were laid on a table, a man holding each of their limbs and their clothing was stripped off. The twine was tightened around their most delicate area and the knife brought down quickly to sever their organs. Honey sealed the wound. The pain would have killed most of them and others just bled to death. It is said that for every 10 boys only one survived. These were the so-called men who served the King. Why a eunuch? They would never marry; would never bother the King's women; could become chamberlains (eunuchs that were on watch in the King's bedchamber never missing anything the King or his concubines did.) If they weren't eunuchs they could impregnate one of them and the King could have thought it was his heir. This was extremely critical if an heir was needed. Thus Hegai had lived a strange life. In his current position he had to of once been a chamberlain. He undoubtedly knew exactly what the King liked both physically and sexually. When Hegai saw Hadassah – not dressed up to impress anyone, embarrassed to be there, his heart suddenly thought, "This one is different; this one stands out!" Then we read in verse 9, "The girl pleased him and won his favor. Immediately he provided her with her beauty treatments and special food. He assigned to her 7 maids selected from the King's palace and moved her and her maids into the best place in the harem." All through the book we will see evidence of the fingerprints of God. Hegai favoring Esther, I believe is one of those times.

In our next session we'll study what really happened in the twelve months of beauty treatments. I think you'll find this research rather fascinating! We'll point our cameras at life in the harem.

Our lesson today: My desire for all of us is when non-Christians look at us they will say, "This one is different; this one stands out and wants to discover why!"

***Persia was a world power, and the King, as the center of that power, was one of the wealthiest people in the world. Persian Kings loved to flaunt their wealth, even wearing precious gemstones in their beards. Jewelry was a sign of rank for Persian men. Even soldiers wore great amounts of gold jewelry into battle" page 994, NIV, Life Application.

Lesson Two Homework

Again, read the entire book of Esther concentrating on yourself as Esther thrown in the middle of hundreds of beautiful women, each thinking she will be Queen and the cat fights, etc. that had to develop. Answer the following, again in first person.

1. You are facing 12 months of beauty treatments (like a year spent at a spa in a large city) but how many hours a day does that take? You'll have hours on your hands while being confined in a harem full of vain virgins – talk about a lion's den! How do you survive?

_____

_____

_____

_____

_____

_____

2. Compare this contest to today's reality shows. How do the girls act around each other when all are vying for the same man?

_____

_____

_____

_____

_____

_____

_____

_____

_____

_____

_____

_____

_____

3. You can select anything you want to wear for your encounter with the king and all you wear will become yours. What do you think you as Esther would select? Can you picture an Esther paper doll?

_____

_____

_____

_____

_____

_____

_____

_____

_____

_____

(Isn't it fun to dream with no budget!)

4. Why would you ask Hegai's advice on your apparel for that evening?

5. Explain how you think you won the favor of everyone who saw you?

_____

_____

_____

_____

_____

_____

_____

_____

_____

_____

_____

_____

_____

_____

6. Now to the hard part: What goes through your mind as you take that one walk from the harem to the king's bedchamber? Remember Esther was human; orphaned; Jewish; terrified!

_____

_____

_____

_____

_____

_____

_____

_____

_____

_____

_____

_____

7.   Why do you think the King picked you?

_____

_____

_____

_____

_____

_____

_____

_____

_____

_____

_____

_____

_____

So pray that as you study this week God will be teaching you the lesson(s) from Esther He has in store for you.

As you will see next week He had a year to prepare Esther for fulfilling His purpose and plan for her life. Are you His captive audience?

Food for thought: Aren't we all preparing to meet the King?

WEEK
Three

READ ESTHER CHAPTER 2

WELL HOW ARE WE DOING PLAYING Esther? Did you enjoy it? Did you journal your answers to the last chapter's homework questions? Did you enjoy your mental trip preparing to meet the King? What color gown would you look best in? How would you style your hair? What jewelry would you select? Necklaces, hair ornaments, earrings, bracelets? Which perfume would you select? Now for the big question! Did you picture what you like or what you think the King would have liked? In, I believe, one of the made-for-TV movies, Scruples, the owner of this specialty store said, when asked how she always dressed so beautifully, "When I dress I realize there's a fine line between sexuality and femininity and I never cross the line." Let's open this evening discussing your answers to Week Two's homework!

To date Esther's life has been a little lonely – no parents – no siblings – reared by an older male – (not the average Jewish family life). Now we see more trauma. A decree has gone out to all the provinces that young virgins were to be taken to the King's harem for the selection of the new queen. The Persian and Medes' mothers of such daughters were in a twitter with excitement in the air as each thought her daughter could be the new queen. They hustled around preparing their daughters for this great event. Every detail from their hair to their wardrobe to their perfumes would have been scrutinized. It is so difficult for me as a mother not to want to shake each of them – as my mom used to say "Until their teeth shattered!" Did they not realize that once their daughters left they would never see them again? Did they not realize they could also be just one of the King's concubines and not his queen?

One idea I have often wrestled with is who turned Esther into the soldiers? Was it a jealous Jewish woman with no daughters thinking the soldiers would give her money if she found a candidate for them? Was it a jealous Jewish man envious of Mordecai who turned her in also for a fee! The Bible never mentions the how of them finding her so we will probably never know!

This reminds me of one of "The Bachelor" shows I watched when the girls were being interviewed about how proud their mothers were of them. How can you be proud to see your daughter flaunt herself on national TV? Then there's Mordecai and Hadassah. <u>She has not had a mother to prepare her for this drastic life change just as those young boys had not been told of their fate as eunuchs!</u> My opinion is that she had no thought that she'd be taken. I truly don't believe she had any idea of her beauty. One book I read said that Hadassah had noticed Mordecai staying up late counting his saved coins and she knew that he was probably thinking of a dowry for her. She had even noticed some rather cute Jewish boys her age when she was in the marketplace and probably was thinking about which one he would chose for her. In reality Mordecai, who worked at the King's Gate and would have known of the search, could have been afraid for Hadassah and was seeing how much money he had to bride the soldiers if they came after her. She is literally kidnapped against Mordecai's will as well as her own. Probably as she is taken away in tears and anguish from her home she clings to her cousin and they both beg the soldiers not to take her. They have so many other girls who want to go. I can even see Mordecai offering every coin he had as a bribe. But a soldier would not have dared to disobey his orders. --- Off she went, thrown into perhaps a wagon or other method of transport – of course being careful not to damage their goods – to the harem of the King.

Those of you who have watched the TV reality show the Bachelor have an idea of what Esther was walking into. Living in an atmosphere of other girls detesting you, belittling you, etc. is not my idea of a fun place. As your scripture states, the year-long prepa- ration period would consist of 6 months of cleansing and softening of the skin and 6 months of cosmetics and adornments. Plus their theory was that in a longer period of time if any of the so-called virgins were with child they would know by then and they could have been killed for not being virgins. You're soon to learn that there was more!

According to my best research, Hadassah's year went something like this:

Upon entering the palace each group of girls would have been taken into a private chamber where each would have been ask to remove all clothing and standing naked their entire bodies would have been inspected for sores or lesions—Persians had a great fear of plagues! Guess all that fanfare of the mom's dressing them up quickly went down the drain. This process would have mortified Hadassah. Once cleared, she would have been taken with the rest of the group to meet the eunuch in charge and in her case this would be Hegai.

Most of the girls were excited to be there and were being awed by the beauty of the King's palace. All of them were thought to be beautiful – many nationalities would be there – and so there were clear cut differences in the girls. All were young and all were supposedly virgins. I can only guess that Hadassah's eyes showed fear, showed modesty, especially in the way she was dressed, with hair not fixed and an everyday dress on and probably even by the sandals she was wearing. The other girls had been sent away in shall we say their Sabbath best.

Hadassah's natural beauty; her not wanting to be noticed; caused Hegai's trained eye to pick her out as unique. We are told she pleased him; she won his favor. (God was already working on His plan for her.) When asked her name, she immediately remembered Mordecai's warning to hide the fact that she was Jewish and we see her begin using the name Esther. But this is a life never dreamed about by Esther – a life of glamour; a life filled with vanity and jealously. As a special favorite of Hegai's, Esther would have been THE target for the other women. History tells stories of girls killed by other girls using everything from poisonous drugs to poisonous snakes purchased by bribing guards.

As this process took several hours it is most likely that the girls were bathed, fed a light dinner, and allowed to sleep prior to the preparation beginning the following day. Once awakened the next morning, if she slept at all, she would have been asked to strip naked in front of her seven maids and Hegai for them to appraise the work ahead of them to turn her into a lady fit to be queen. As Esther's feet would have been calloused from walking in sandals on dirt roads and her hands chapped from washing clothes and preparing grain for bread, they had their hands full and they knew it. She would have been placed in a huge tub where every inch of her body would be scrubbed. Then the worst for her in the first phase of her preparation was when all her body hair would have been removed. One account said, "and even the hair from her sacred places would be shaved." This was a painful process, and I can't even imagine how embarrassing for a girl who had never even lived with other women (no church camps with no shower curtains). This process, she was told when she was protesting, was to prepare her skin for the king's touch. Something that also shocked me was that she could have elected to have her head shaved as wigs were used a great deal of the time. Hadassah's long, black, shiny hair kept them from insisting that she also follow this ritual.

Every day after, all the women would be bathed morning and night with oil of myrrh. They would eat a diet normally at their young age to assist in filling them out to be more "womanly". She had no choice but to eat all portions of food set before her and no more. One dish that would have started most meals was a soup described as thick green sludge with waxy fat beans floating like dead fish in the river and an odor to match. But then there was usually a spicy rice dish and perhaps roasted lamb. Probably Esther had never tasted much lamb if any at all. She and Mordecai probably raised them to sale but probably could not have afforded them to eat for just the two of them. They may have eaten them on the Jewish holidays. So here we have Esther, alone, having been mortified, stripped naked, shaved, just a teen eating out of gold and silver dishes, with 7 maids and sleeping in the King's palace and not just thrown in with the other girls but as you read this week she was "in the best place in the harem."

Every morning she would be awakened early, propped up in bed with a tray of tea and fruits; servants would enter with steaming towels and between sips towels are laid on her face, bosom and hands. History said, "It was a very gentle way to wake up."

Every evening servants would lead her to bed where they would slather her in oils and creams (nightly embalming) – used many different oils but myrrh was the favorite. Myrrh was placed on her face sometimes mixed with almond oil; lotus oil for her bosom; myrrh on hands and rest of body. Then she would have been wrapped in strips of clean linen and laid on her back – hands at sides, for the night. Preparation never allowed for a girl to even rub her eyes or she might wrinkle the skin around them. A servant stood guard over Esther every night to be sure she did not turn in bed which would crease the body nor allow her to rub her eyes and wrinkle her facial area. That's why steaming towels are used in the morning – to remove embalming oils from the previous night and to steep the skin in mystic power. If a girl complained of a headache their remedy was the rubbing of oil on their temples made from rose petals and a dead baby cobra floating in it. I would think there were few complaints.

Persian healers and magicians would visit girls on a regular basis to feel their bellies to determine if they were fertile and smelled their breath to know what humor they were in.

Now to the crucial training – she would have had a special instructor of seduction – private lessons (very private and very mortifying for Esther). These were only given to the women Hegai (or whomever was the head eunuch in a certain harem) thought could be selected. So, she would have to have:

(1) learned how to disrobe in front of the King
(2) learned seductive dance(s)

(3) been taught how to capture his mind – tanta-
lize him (sounds like a mental giant.)
(4) been taught never to use her full voice when
speaking – slow and soft like a gentle fragrance
and how to walk as if gliding on pure air.
(5) been taught to be anointed in the most unlikely
places with perfume made from lotus flowers
set in oil from a crocodile (aphrodisiac).

Next came the time of experimenting with cosmetics and adorations. Esther's maids would have tried
every color combination on her lips and around her
eyes. Every hair style would have been fashioned. Most
harems – and I'm sure King Xerxes had one – had a
treasury and the girls would have been led in there
to select the adornments they wished to wear. This
would have been done probably in the last month so
that hair adoration and jewels to enhance their gowns
could be chosen. Most of the girls were said to be so
weighted down with jewels they needed help walking
as they were allowed to keep everything they wore that
night. Gowns and fabrics of all colors and fabrics were
shown. No girl would have any excuse for not looking
her very best.

So for 12 months Esther was bathed twice daily, slathered in oils and wrapped nightly, fed to round her out in just the right places; body shaved on a routine basis; checked for her menstrual period; hair fixed and twisted; cosmetics put on and off daily, etc. Selections, selections, selections!

In the midst of all of this new life Esther was confronted daily with hatred, spite, name calling, belittling, etc. If you listened outside the walls you would have heard the cat meows and the claws being sharpened! So life was not as she had dreamed. This was no Miss America contest; this was no gold medal at the Olympics although she had been trained like one. This was leading up to her night with the King.

Now for a brief break before I share what I think happened on Esther's night with the King. Let's look at your homework questions in realm of what I've said tonight. What goes through your mind as you take that long walk from the harem to the King's bedchamber? Remember Esther was human; orphaned, Jewish, terrified! What would have been the hardest part of the year for you? Did Esther continue to be different from the other girls? Do you think she slept with the King? Remember this is all opinion and yours is as good as mine.

Now for my story – you can write yours!

My modesty intrigued Hegai. As he watched me daily he began to see that I was truly just who I was. There seemed to be no vanity; no greed; no whining; no fits of rage; no need to be number 1. He befriended me and just as I had done with Mordecai I confided in him. I was used to asking Mordecai his opinion and thus I listened to Hegai (who had once been the King's chamberlain). By the time 12 months were coming to an end, however, Hegai sat down with me and explained the significance of my time with the King! He emphasized I had no choice. I could either choose to follow his every instruction to be queen or live the rest of my life in a concubine making sure I knew which choice was best! He told me that since he had favored me his position was at stake if I was not selected. He wore me down with the guilt of letting him down when he had so befriended me. He gave me no choice but to follow his every command to become Queen. All the king's servants – no matter their status – lived in fear of upsetting the King.

When I first arrived in Hegai's harem, I had no prior opinions of Persian fashion, hairstyles, protocol – I only knew how to live in a Godly fashion and obey Jewish law as taught me by Mordecai. Oh, how I miss him today! I had learned to trust only Hegai just as I had done so many years with Mordecai. Every decision would have begun with which do you like best, Hegai, and he would have informed me that it wasn't what he liked but what the king would like and that my preparation had to be to please the King. After all, pleasing the King was Hegai's lifetime duty!

As the days grew shorter, I began to pray daily for a word from God to help me in this situation. Mordecai would also have been praying. Finally, the day would come when knowing there was no way out, I would have to prepare for my night with the King. I followed Hegai's every suggestion except for one. I have chosen the sheerest white shimmering fabric and lapis blue satin trim I could find. At least I would lose my virginity in the colors I would have worn had I been betrothed to a young Jewish lad. I knew Hegai would not allow the selection of a plainer fabric. In my society both the bride and groom would wear white trimmed in blue on their wedding day denoting humility and devotion. (White wedding gowns did not become *en vogue* until late in the 15th Century. But the blue trim tradition continued with our "something blue".) It's a small token to me as I am laid on the altar of a pagan king or should I say bed? How immature of me to even have dreamed my life could have been spared from this evening? Hegai at first frowned on my selection. He knew exactly what would please the King but for the first time I was able to convince him that my idea would add even more mystery to what lies beneath the gown! Plus he loved the design of the dress and especially how it flowed as I walked. I think I've toughened up a little having to deal with the other girls for a year. With Hegai's permission the only jewelry I wore that night was a necklace which was shaped like the flower called myrtle, the root of my name. My skin was now as soft as any humans could have been: my hair shined like never before and my eyes had been made to look like diamonds shining through a black abyss. My so-called God given beauty was allowed to show through as I presented myself to the King. There is no doubt that I carried myself in the stately fashion Hegai had taught me, but my legs were wobbling like a newborn colt's. I was shocked as I left the harem when the other girls began gasping at my beauty. "And Esther won the favor of everyone who saw her." (Esther 2:15b) Hegai took my arm and escorted me to the King's entrance. He truly seemed proud of the results of his challenge. Now, however, it is time for me to be on my own as he escorts me into the King's bedchamber where the king's guards will be in charge.

As I enter the King's bedchamber I am shocked. I had never seen the King before and thought he would have been much older. He sat staring at me as I swallowed several times. He asked me to enter and then stood laughing at me blushing.

"Modesty is new to me." He says as he circles around me looking me over from head to foot. "Is one necklace all you chose to wear when most come to me hardly able to stand for the weight of their bounty?"

I am now totally scared to death! I am so attempting to remember everything at once that Hegai taught me so I take a deep breath and softly answer, "Oh, this is not for me, my King. This is a gift for you to remember me by." I slowly take it off straining to keep my hands from shaking as I hand him the necklace."

The King begins laughing again. "A gift for me who can have anything in the kingdom he so choses?

– A gift taken from my own treasury? A gift to a man who spends his days accepting gifts from all over the world as I'm expected to solve the problems of their province. Look at all these scrolls I have to read filled with requests from distant nations. I really want for nothing but peace of mind and they think a gift can get their answer."

I have really irritated him and am failing Hegai. Then I remembered how Mordecai loved for me to read to him when he came home troubled by news within the Jewish neighborhood or at the King's gate where he worked. "My King, if I have troubled you perhaps I could read to you and soothe your mind." – maybe a great stalling routine?

Again he laughs. "You think you have come here to read to me?" Then he paused and turned to me, "Who taught you to read anyway?"

Gulping down my fear I softly reply, "As an orphan I was raised by an older cousin with no children and he taught me to read and write like he would have a son."

The King shockingly takes my hand guiding me over to an outer patio that overlooks the city of Susa. Still staring at me he asked, "What's your name?"

"They call me Esther."

"Well, Esther, you see all that land and all those people – yes, I'm their King but I have to also guard and protect them and sometimes they have more problems than I can bear."

"Yes, King Xerxes" using his name for the first time, "but by putting their welfare first the people love and serve you."

"Who do you love and serve Esther?" mused the King.

"I love my God." I stated very softly as I was greatly afraid my answer would offend him.

"Why?" asked the King.

"Because I know He only wants what is best for me."

"And is being here with me what's best for you?" Again he smiles at my naivety!

Bowing my head, I just say nothing! That was not part of Hegai's script.

The King then lifts my chin and a tear starts its journey down my cheek. "This God of yours, Esther, must have great wisdom. What would His desire be for you?"

I walked away and pretended to look across the city attempting to buy time and pray that God will put the right words in my mouth. "My God's wish for me is for me to be obedient to Him."

Coming up behind me he says, "And is sleeping with the King obedience?"

"To sleep with a man outside of marriage is not" I whispered and again bowing my head I wondered how in the world did this conversation get started? The King sits down on a huge lounge and again looks me up and down.

"But what if you were married to the man, is that being obedient? Would that make your God happy?"

For the first time I got the nerve to look squarely in his eyes. Again, tears spill down my cheeks and I have to turn quickly around to hide them. Tears were not part of my training; I knew Hegai would not be pleased with me! I was just so absorbed with emotion and fear that I couldn't hold them back. The King walked around to face me, shook his head at my tears, took my hand and led me over to the shelves full of scrolls.

"Read to me, Esther, like you used to read to your guardian" and he pulled out a scroll, led me over to his bed where he reclined as he motioned for me to sit by his side as I read. This was way too close to him I thought to myself. But I cleared my throat, unrolled the scroll and was shocked to see that the story he had chosen was one of Mordecai's favorites. I relaxed a little and read it to the King as I had many times for Mordecai. It seemed to be just as soothing for the King. As I finished the story, however, the King sat up, snapped his fingers and immediately one of his guards, called the Immortals, appeared. I am frozen with fear. I thought I had done what he asked. To my amazement, King Xerxes tells the guard to take care of me as he just remembered some business he had to take care of immediately. Almost as quickly as he left the room a servant appeared with a tray of fruit and tea for me. Hegai had warned me not to eat unless I had to while with the King as food could affect my breath so I refused nicely.

The evening was getting later and I mentally dwelt on what lie ahead. I walked back out to the patio overlooking Susa and thought of Mordecai. Do you know where I am tonight? Are you disappointed in me? I am with myself. I stood looking out and began praying for him that he would be able to take the money the commissioners gave him for me and added to the coins he had saved he could marry. I prayed that God would continue to look after Mordecai as I would if I was with him. Sooner than I thought, King Xerxes reappeared. He seemed preoccupied.

"Esther" he said. "I'm sorry but something has come up and I need to get a decree out immediately. I was ready to call the scribes back in but then I remembered that you said you could write. Could you help me here?"

This night was becoming stranger than even I had imagined – not at all like Hegai had said it would. "Of course, my King, if you so desire."

King Xerxes escorted me to a large desk-like table where a servant was arranging papyrus and some writing utensils. I was motioned to take a seat. My hands were shaking and I was thinking, is this a test to see if I can really write?' Positioning myself on the chair, I looked up at him - wondering what to write.

"Esther, can I dictate it to you?" he asked.

"Yes," I replied, "if it pleases you."

The King walked behind me and started: "I, King Xerxes I, on this day in the year 479, (pause) do issue a royal decree to all the nobles of the provinces, (pause) the satraps, the governors and the King's administration (pause) and to all people living within my 127 provinces, (pause again to let me catch up and moves in front of the desk bending down as if to check my writing.) He then looks straight into my eyes (I don't think I can keep calm much longer.) and continues …."that I have selected Esther to be my queen."

At that I turned and looked astonished at the King. He brought me quickly to my feet, put his arms around me, and held me so close I thought I'd smother. Then he tipped my chin one more time and said, "No more tears, Queen Esther, they're not befitting a queen." At a snap of his fingers, 7 female servants appeared.

He softly speaks to me now in more of an official manner, "They will escort you to your new living quarters and serve you as Queen. I will add to the decree that a royal coronation will begin in 7 days where I will publicly crown you queen" – and with a grin he whispers in my ear, "and make your god happy."

"Hegai will assist you in the preparations." He pauses for a few minutes looking me over from head to toe one more time and then he takes me again in his arms just hugging me almost like a father does a playful child, but it allowed me time to take in the situation. Then turning my face up to his he continues, "After the coronation I will expect you to enter my bedchamber as my wife. Can you do that for me without tears?"

Attempting to breath and thank God at the same time, I looked King Xerxes in the face, and to his (and my) amazement, I took his face in my hands and gently whispered, "Yes, my King." Kissing him on the forehead, "Whatever, pleases you."

A huge smile comes across his face and he whispers in my ear, "You had better exit now with the servants or I won't wait that long." I began to turn to leave when he continues, "Oh, and Esther tell Hegai he was right. Your beauty is much more than skin deep. Your very presence refreshed my entire being."

Blushingly smiling I turned and followed the servants out of the king's bedchamber where I see Hegai waiting for me with his arm extended to accompany me to my private quarters and the beginning of my new world. I have never seen Hegai smile like this and I had never felt God's presence like I do tonight!

I hope you can see in my story that in order to visualize what could have happened we have to establish perimeters. We have to think on his and her cultures. We have to remember that he has now been King for 7 years and we hope has matured and Esther has been in preparation for a year allowing her to mature. We need to remember that this King has had women in and out of his bedchamber on a nightly basis purely for sexual purposes. So who does he talk to? Who does he have to share his life? Who truly cares if he lives or dies? With Esther he had someone who could read to him; who seemed to understand the pressures of governing his empire; someone who actually blushed and shed tears. AND of course who was most beautiful! We have to remember that God is positioning Esther, a woman, to save the Jewish nation. Could God break His own rules to win? I think not! The "Holy How" that Esther represented here had to be special. She had to be and act like a child of God. In my mind God just couldn't have let her spend the night with the King – He found a way out just like He had for the Israelites escaping Egypt when He parted the Red Sea; like He did for Abraham when he thought he was sacrificing his only son and there's a ram; like He did when He sent His Son to die on a cross but provided an empty tomb! If you're faithful to Him, He'll be faithful to us and Esther knew that night that God had intervened. Yes, she still married a man with many women but remember she was the Godly one here and he is still the pagan! God allowed her to marry and remain faithful to one man. What a lesson, ladies, for all of us.

Well, did you conclude how you think Esther's night with the King would have occurred? Where did you differ with me? Let's discuss!

We need to briefly discuss the episodes found in Chapter 2:19-20 and 21-23.

First, we have the issue of verse 19, "when the virgins were assembled a second time" – your thoughts here? Were these the virgins that never got an audience with the King because he selected Esther? What happened to them? Did they go back home or were they just transferred to the concubine harem? No one knows. My feeling would be that they were transferred to the other harem. Verse 20 is self-explanatory.

Then verses 21-23, which are normally submitted: Mordecai uncovers a conspiracy – another God thing! Mordecai's job was basically to sit at the king's gate and be a scribe. While there he overhears the plot – which emphasizes the fact that to date still no one knows Esther is Jewish or of any relationship to Mordecai as stated in vs. 20 or they wouldn't have allowed him to overhear the plot. It also tells us that Mordecai continues to be able to communicate to Esther. We also know that Esther was perhaps at this time in her marriage in constant companionship to the King because she told him of the plot without fear of her life. We know the King investigated, found Mordecai's information to be true and the eunuchs were hanged. Why didn't the King immediately reward Mordecai? Historians say they think it was because he left for battle or to another palace, etc. but we know the answer: another God thing!

Chapter 3 goes into the entire plot by Haman to destroy the Jews. Isn't it great to now be Queen! Can you sense the relief, the sense of complete trust in your God?

This week's lesson: Be patient – God is always here for us!

Lesson Three Homework

This week take the place of Mordecai making the decision to kneel or not to kneel and an even greater tragedy, facing the condemnation of his race to death!

1. Think about the fact that Haman has now risen above the king's 7 princes as second in command. Why?

_____

_____

_____

_____

_____

_____

_____

_____

_____

_____

2. Mordecai refused to kneel – what are the consequences and what other example of this type of godliness do you remember from the O.T?

_____

_____

_____

_____

_____

_____

_____

_____

_____

_____

_____

_____

_____

_____

_____

3. Why does Haman hate the Jews? What significance does the term, "the Agagite" have to do with his hatred?

_____

_____

_____

_____

_____

_____

_____

_____

_____

_____

_____

_____

_____

_____

4. What was Haman's convincing proposition to King Xerxes?

_____

_____

_____

_____

_____

_____

_____

_____

_____

_____

_____

_____

_____

5. What exactly did Haman's decree, sealed by the king's signet ring, say?

_____

_____

_____

_____

_____

_____

_____

_____

_____

_____

_____

_____

_____

_____

6. What significance is the casting of lots?

_____

_____

_____

_____

_____

_____

_____

_____

_____

_____

_____

_____

_____

_____

_____

7. Picture yourself with the news, tearing off your clothes and donning sackcloth and ashes and walking through downtown (in your city) wailing? Have you ever faced a situation like that? I hope not!

_____

_____

_____

_____

_____

_____

_____

_____

_____

_____

_____

_____

8. How does Mordecai convince Esther to intercede?

_____

_____

_____

_____

_____

_____

_____

_____

_____

_____

_____

_____

_____

_____

_____

9. What was Esther's request once she agreed to risk her life?

_____

_____

_____

_____

_____

_____

_____

_____

_____

_____

_____

_____

_____

10. Back to our "God thing" in 2:21-23. How does God use this to call attention to the Jewish people at this time of travail? Is He not awesome? Haman was his own worst enemy! Second in command was not enough for him.

_____

_____

_____

_____

_____

_____

_____

_____

_____

_____

_____

_____

_____

11. What lesson do you think God is teaching YOU with this part of Esther?

_____

_____

_____

_____

_____

_____

_____

_____

_____

_____

_____

_____

_____

_____

WEEK
Four

READ CHAPTERS 3/4/5

IS THIS NOT A HUMBLING STUDY? Esther was willing to risk her life; Mordecai was willing to risk his life and both lived with the fear of their race being annihilated! What are we willing to risk? Makes me feel so unworthy!

(God knew King Xerxes better than Hegai did!)

In your last session you had been crowned queen and just as an added comment about your coronation – according to historical accounts this would have been at the main capital in Persepolis. We know Mordecai had discovered the plot against the king and now we meet

Haman! Haman, son of Hammedatha, the Agagite! Why was this description of Haman so important to our understanding of his hatred for the Jews? "Why did Haman want to destroy all Jews just because of one man's action? (1) Haman was an Agagite (3:1), a descendent of Agag, king of the Amalekites (I Samuel 15:20) The Amalekites were ancient enemies of the Israelites (see Exodus 17:16; Deuteronomy 25:17-19). Haman's hatred was directed not just at Mordecai, but to all Jews. (2) As second-in-command in the Persian Empire (3:1) Haman loved his power and authority and the reverence shown him. The Jews, however, looked to God as their final authority, not to any man. Haman realized that the only way to fulfill his self-centered desires was to kill all those who disregarded his authority. His quest for personal power and his hatred of the Jewish race consumed him, etc." (Footnote on page 999 in my Life Application NIV Bible) If you answered this just tell me the scripture you used! To truly understand you'd have to go all the way back to I Samuel 15. Let's turn there and read.

The Amalekites were a band of guerrilla terrorists. They lived by attacking other nations and carrying off their wealth and their families. They were the first to attack the Israelites as they entered the Promised Land, and they continued to raid Israelite camps at every opportunity. Not only were they deadly but their corrupt, idolatrous religious practices were a threat to God's people SO God directed Saul to give the following command in I Samuel 15:3. Is this what the Israelites did? NO! We can say "Oh, Saul, how could you have done such a thing?" but we disobey every day, don't we? Saul chose selective obedience which is just another form of disobedience. So Samuel went to Saul chastising him for disobedience, Saul attempted to lie out of it – like you can lie to God and Him not know. Let's take an extra minute and read Samuel's words in verses 22-23. Then Samuel has King Agag brought before him and say: verse 33: "As your sword has made women childless; so will your mother be childless among women" and he puts Agag to death. (Note: Saul became King in 1050) Now we meet Haman, a descendent of King Agag whose family was killed by the Jews. (Note: Check Deut. 25:17-19 and Ex. 17:16) to understand Mordecai's dislike for the Amalekites.) Interesting thought with no factual answer: if all women were killed where did Haman come from? (Another fingerprint of God's?) Anyway

Haman's hatred and prejudice hidden in his heart became his downfall as we watch God's plan unfold in the 12th year of King Xerxes' reign.

Now let's start at verse one. Why was Haman so promoted – 2nd in the kingdom where once the 7 princes of Persia were 2nd? History tells us that Haman fought at Xerxes' side in the battle and had won his reputation as a warrior. In fact some books say he commanded not only the Immortals that guarded the King but also the entire army and in so doing had trained his troops to plunder wherever they went and that he had collected a fortune. This was the reason he could offer to pay the king 10,000 talents (about 375 tons of silver) and other commentators said he planned to make the 10,000 when the Jews were killed and their homes plundered.

One interesting side note to add here is that the Immortals wore highly decorated uniforms which distinguished them. One author said that Haman's dislike for the Jews was evident even then as they wore a crooked cross on their uniforms to set them apart. This crooked cross resembled the one we know as the Swastika. In the History of the Swastika it is defined as an ancient symbol that has been used for over 3000 years – even predates the ancient Troy showing that the swastika was a commonly used symbol as far back as 1000 BCE. It was said to represent life, sun, power, strength, and good luck. However, Haman could not have used the symbol for his hatred as until World War II no such meaning accompanied the symbol. During WWI it was even used on shoulder patches of the American 45ᵗʰ Division and on the Finnish Air Force until after WWII.

As I said in lesson one, Xerxes trusted Haman with his life. In verse 2 we find out that due to his position all royal officials at the king's gate were to bow and pay honor to Haman but Mordecai could not bow to anyone but His God. Plus he knew about the treatment of the Israelites and this perhaps created a greater dislike for men of this race. We continue to worship idols today, don't we? Verses 3-5 are self-explanatory but we are told in verse 4 that Mordecai had confessed he was a Jew. What really angered Haman? "Haman looked for a way to destroy all Mordecai's people, the Jews." What did Haman do to determine when "his gods" thought he should annihilate the Jews! Loved the timing! It gave Esther almost another year to mature in her faith and her relationship with the

King. Lots were cast on the 1st month but Jews were not to be killed until the 12th month. Interesting aside – lots were also cast at the foot of the cross.

Then Haman persuaded Xerxes (a man who paid no attention to details) to have these people killed:

a) whose customs are different
b) who do not obey the king's laws (not singular like not bowing down to Haman)
c) not in the King's best interest to tolerate them
d) and if so I will personally finance this great victory with 10,000 talents of silver.

What was the King's reaction to strange, disobedient people in his land? He gave his signet ring to Haman to seal the decree. Did you ever have a friend like Haman that you trusted to this point only to be totally betrayed?

Thus, in verses 12-15 we see the decree is sent out; the Jews are bewildered; and the King and Haman sit down to "have a drink!" They might say today, "to have a beer or a cocktail"!

Moving in to chapter 4: Mordecai's reaction and Esther's reply. Mordecai reacted like any good Jew just as Jacob did when he learned that Joseph was supposedly dead – he tore his clothes and put on sackcloth and applied ashes (signs of mourning much like wearing black is today; ashes or dust sign of what they would become) and went about the city wailing!

In order to understand this type of grief you would have to have received an edict from our President ordering all Christians, men, women, children (including infants) to be killed in 12 months! Sometimes I feel that's the judgment being handed down to us from the world. Why don't all Christians either die or just hide themselves in their churches where they're of no competition. Let's bury them with their God! I tell my ladies that Christians didn't come out of their closets soon enough!

Thus we know the Jews had a year's warning. Do you think any of them escaped—just packed up and faced the robbers on the roads back to Jerusalem? Next we see (verses 4-5) Esther heard of Mordecai's strange behavior and sent a eunuch to see what is wrong. (Isn't it funny how staffs talked even back then or how else could Esther have learned this news?) Verses 6-8 inform Esther of exactly what had happened. Her people have been condemned to death; she is their only hope; she must go before the King and beg for mercy – pleading for her people! What was Esther's reply? Read verse 11

–Then we get Mordecai's reply – the famous "you were born for such a time as this." Quickly check your time-frame given to you at the beginning of the study: In what year of Xerxes' reign did this plot occur? 12th year of his reign and he and Esther had now been married 5 years, and she perhaps was 20 by now.

Look closely at verse 15 ~ when my total admiration for Esther rises to its highest level. She may be queen but she's also a Jew condemned to death; she knows it; she asked for 3 days of fasting and I believe "prayer" and then she'll be willing to go before the King even if it means death, "if I perish, I perish." (Many male scholars are so critical of the book of Esther because God's name is never mentioned but here we have a Jewish lady facing death with the wisdom to take 3 days of fasting prior to her decision.)

In all accounts I've read, fasting by the Jews is always combined with praying. When we attempt to take things into our own hands, without first presenting our trouble to the Lord, we deserve to fail. Now for an interesting and often overlooked little phrase, "I and my maids will fast with you." Had her maids converted? Talk about lifestyle evangelism. Esther practiced it many years ago! Does that not make a statement of who Esther really is to you? No Jew would have asked "Pagans" to fast (and I believe pray) with them! Would you want a non-believer by your side at ~such a time as this? Have you won 7 women to Christ? I will give you a little slack and say her servants were a captive audience.

Esther's position as Queen even in 5 years had not changed her faith – if anything it had strengthened it! She loved God! He was still her Number 1 King! She knows He's the one that truly made her Queen.

Now for an interesting scenario for you! Esther's maids and her eunuch now knew Esther is a Jew – believe they had known earlier but now Mordecai has verified the fact to all around her! They also would have known about Haman's hatred for the Jews and that as a wealthy, shall we say Prime Minister of Persia, he would have paid dearly to know that fact. What do you think kept them from turning her in? Remember the King did not even know yet. Give great thought to this in light of today's political scene.

Chapter 5 begins another long walk for our Esther! This time the King's not waiting for her in his bedchamber. This time she's walking alone, having not eaten in three days, probably not having slept much, drained from planning a banquet that would woe even a King, dressed much like her preparation had taught her 5 years ago, praying with each step for her God's presence and His great wisdom "for such a time as this." This time it's a life or death situation. Not only is her life in his hands but the lives of her people. There are pictures of kings then with bodyguards standing around them with axe-like long swords ready to slay anyone who enters the King's presence without permission. I'm certain Esther was quite aware of how her life could be taken.

To add to the drama, scripture says, the King had not called her to his bed for 30 days and we're not told why. Perhaps he was just consumed with running his empire; had a new concubine that he fancied; was gone; whatever but what we do know is "when he saw Queen Esther standing in the court, he was pleased with her…" Things have not changed ladies! All husbands want you to want them! King Xerxes knew his own law! He knew she was risking her life! All men like mystery in their women and what could be more mysterious than wanting to know what would cause a Queen to risk her life to be with you. He's thinking she's really missed me! Another God thing that hasn't changed! So the golden scepter was lowered; she touched the end, and approached the King. If her legs had been wobbly, her heart throbbing, her prayers never ceasing on her first meeting with the King with her virginity at stake; how much more would this walk have taken courage with the risk of losing her life and the lives of all the Jews! WOW! Talk about a Holy How - she was God's chosen one "for such a time as this." Esther could have failed by allowing her fear to keep her from the mission and God would just have used another vessel. Just like us. This is an important lesson for us to remember: when we fail to follow His plan for our lives our joy will be given to someone else.

It always makes me smile when I read verse 3 – the King was so excited that he even offered her up to half his kingdom! He was saying to his guards and anyone else in the King's hall, my queen risked her life to meet with me and I'll reward her with up to half my kingdom!

Esther continues the mystery. She doesn't immediately make her request known. God has not nudged her in that way. She just says in a voice so soft it fills the room like a fragrance (taught to her years ago by Hegai), "If it pleases the King, let the King together with Haman, come to the banquet I have prepared." How difficult it must have been for her to postpone his answer to her petition and to even think of including Haman in her plans!

She goes to the Number 3 male loving gesture, food. Esther says she has prepared a banquet – a banquet for him. Ladies, that's like inviting the King to a picnic in bed! The King, still excited, immediately orders Haman to be brought in to attend. The King is eager shall we say and I love that about him. With hundreds of women to choose from on a nightly basis he still loved Esther, his beautiful inside and out queen! And I'm sure he could hardly wait for dessert!

So the King and Haman attended the banquet. At the back of this study I have outlined for you how to stage King Xerxes' banquet for you and the women in your study. We did this and it was so exciting! The only item we could not find to enjoy was "breast of hummingbird" – a delicacy at that time.

I can just see the King eating with his queen lying by his side popping perhaps grapes or strawberries into his mouth and he asked again. "Now what is your petition and again he offers her half his kingdom in front of Haman. I can just see Haman swallowing hard as he lives in fear that she'll take it. Haman was greedy, power hungry, and I'm certain would not have been the least bit negative about assassinating the King if the right plot was presented. He didn't want Esther in his way – which is ironic as he doesn't know she's Jewish and he's trying to kill her anyway.

Again God has not directed Esther to present her petition so once more and in her softest, sexiest voice says, "if it pleases the King to grant my petition and fulfill my request, let the King and Haman come tomorrow to the banquet I will prepare for them. Then I will answer the King's question." Xerxes is thinking not only does she want me tonight but she wants to be sure she's with me again tomorrow night!

More mystery! More tantalizing eyes feasting on him; savoring him with rich foods and wine in a most romantic setting! You know the Queen's staff has gone all out for this occasion. They were probably shocked however to be told we're doing a repeat tomorrow night. Their creative juices had to really be flowing and I think they were spiritually filled!

So we see second-in-command Haman almost beside himself with pride and vanity. He could hardly wait to get home and tell his wife and wine-drinking friends. On his way, however, God placed a stumbling block – Mordecai! Did you ever have a super time to only get home and one of your parents down-plays your excitement or you call a friend to say so and so asked you out or you'd had a great first date and their meowing in the other end of the phone almost burst your bubble? Well Haman was "filled with rage." In fact his boiling rage was bubbling over! But then he got home and began his nightly bragging – about his vast wealth, his 10 sons (many), and his promotion by the king to #2 in command, and then he tells them about his evening with the king and his wife – like a private dinner with our President and his wife! I so hope we have better friends to share our good times with than Haman did. After the brag-fest, Haman cannot contain his anger any longer and spews out the incident with Mordecai (5:13). His wife and friends suggest a gallows be built. Not just any gallows but one 75 foot high so all of Susa could see what happens to anyone who doesn't bow to Haman! Isn't God amazing like the saying that 'he hung himself with his own rope'! So he had a plan! Have the gallows built, gain Xerxes's permission, hang Mordecai, and go to the Queen's banquet the following evening and be happy! We know whose plan is being fulfilled! Haman's judgment scene is unfolding as we speak!

Let me add here my notes about Haman's gallows. Historical accounts tell us that the normal punishment in that era was for the convicted person to be impaled on a pole and his body left there to be eaten by the birds. Thus most accounts say that would have been the type of gallows built. Remember being taught about mountains and valleys in our lives? Well Haman is about to make a quick descent in more ways than one! Shall we say - to a home hotter even than in Iran.

In our next session we tackle chapters 6 & 7 where Mordecai will be honored and Haman will be hanged! We will see God's plan come to fruition!

*The Jews numbered 15 million out of the 100 million in the Persian Empire. Thus they were, shall we say, outnumbered! I read once though that "One with God is a majority"!

Lesson Four Homework

1. God's name is never mentioned in the book of Esther. Is He there? List the ways in which you know the spirit of God was moving in each chapter, 1-7:

_____

_____

_____

_____

_____

_____

_____

_____

_____

_____

_____

_____

2. Now for meditation time: Look at your life –
yes, your entire life. List the ways you know
the spirit of God was/is moving in your life.
Reflect on the times you thought He was
absent. Then give God the glory for loving you
as you become quiet in His presence searching
for His purpose and plan for your life. You are
no different than Esther. Your purpose and
plan may not be to save a nation, but I can
guarantee you that God has a plan for YOU,
and you will not be at peace until you find it
and obey it.

_____

_____

_____

_____

_____

_____

_____

3. See how quickly you can recall the facts to date, giving chapter and verse:

a). Esther's Jewish name is _____ ,

Chapter _____ ,

Verse _____

b). Mordecai is Esther's _____ ,

Chapter , _____

Verse _____ ,

c). Esther's father's name is _____ ,,

Chapter _____ ,

Verse _____

d). Queen Vashti was asked to appear at the king's banquet wearing , _____

_____

Chapter _____ ,

Verse _____

e). Her disobedience led to her being _____ ,

_____

Chapter _____ ,

Verse _____

f). The king's advisors were also called _____

_____

at the time of the 180-day banquet,

Chapter _____ ,

Verse _____

g). _____

replaced the king's 2nd in command,

Chapter _____ ,

Verse _____

h). Haman's wife's name is _____ ,

Chapter _____ ,

Verse _____

i). Hegai was a _____ ,

in charge of the king's harem, Chapter _ ,

Verse _____

j). Mordecai warned Esther not to mention

her _____ ,

Chapter _____ ,

Verse _____

k). How long would Esther be in the harem

in preparation to meet the king?

_____

Chapter _____ ,

Verse _____

4. Explain this verse: "Since Mordecai, before whom your downfall started, is of Jewish origin, you cannot stand against him – you will surely come to ruin!"

_____

_____

_____

_____

_____

_____

_____

_____

_____

_____

_____

_____

_____

_____

5. Now I want you to be a detective. What events in the book of Esther do you think will come back to haunt King Xerxes before he dies? His death is not mentioned but he has already made two tragic mistakes. You already know that the heir to the throne, Artaxerxes, succeeds Xerxes. (Love to make you think – hint: this is your author' opinion ~ not scripture!)

_____

_____

_____

_____

_____

_____

_____

_____

_____

_____

WEEK
Five

READ CHAPTERS 6, 7, 8

GOD IS ALWAYS AT WORK. CHAPTER 6 opens with the king tossing and turning, not being able to sleep. He had spent the evening with Queen Esther, had eaten a large rich meal and now he was 'sleepless in Susa'. What better way to make yourself sleepy than to read official documents? We know he didn't start with the beginning of his reign or they would have been there several days to get to the plot on his life that was reported by Mordecai. When he had read the account, the king asked his attendant, "What honor and recognition has Mordecai received

for this?" The answer "Nothing has been done for him."
Have you ever been blessed by someone but were too
busy at the time to say thank you? Well, the king was
not pleased with that answer but not wanting to act
without advice asked, "Who is in the court?" We know
that it has to be early morning by this time as Haman
had just entered the court in an attempt to get the king
to grant him the thrill of hanging Mordecai. I imagine
Haman had been up all night also planning his revenge.
Again, God was at work building the tool by which to
rid the Jews of the evil Haman.

Xerxes I'm sure, was glad it was Haman his 2ⁿᵈ
in command, and asked that he be brought in. I love
this question: "What should be done for the man the
king delights to honor?" Can you not see the smile on
Haman's face as his chest swells to almost bursting?
The king has to be thinking of him. After all, he's the
one who had enjoyed the private banquet with just the
king and queen. He's the one Xerxes made 2ⁿᵈ in command above the 7 Princes of Persia. We are allowed
at this time to read Haman's thoughts. Verse 6b says,
"Now Haman thought to himself, 'Who is there that
the king would rather honor than me?'" Boy are those
puffed up words right from the heart of an evil one! I

couldn't help but think that sometime earlier Haman must have envisioned himself being honored as was evident in his response to the king. "Have them bring a royal robe the king has worn and a horse the king has ridden, one with a royal crest placed on its head. Then let the robe and horse be entrusted to one of the king's most noble princes (someone under Haman). Let them robe the man the king delights to honor and lead him on the horse through the city streets, proclaiming before him, "This is what is done for the man the king delights to honor." Can't you just imagine that God planted that vision in Haman's head to be used against him because Haman would have bought into that idea in the wink of an eye! God is always at work! Now to the bubble bursting, blood draining from one's face moment of truth! Haman is to do exactly as Haman said BUT for Mordecai! Did you not just want to burst out in Hallelujahs! I believe Haman's proclamation of "This is what is done for the man the king delights to honor" may have been a little weak. What about you?

Nothing is said about Mordecai's reaction to this honor. We know he did as Haman had requested (can't you just visualize this scene of Haman who hated

Mordecai having to inform Mordecai of the king's decision? Can't you just imagine Haman's mortification while he's parading Mordecai around – Mordecai who should have been hanging from the gallows was riding on the king's horse and it was Haman's suggested honor.) I love the method God has of twisting our lemons into lemonade, don't you? All we know is that Mordecai rode the horse adorned in the king's robe and verse 12 says he returned to the king's gate. In other words he went back to work. If Mordecai is who I think he is he would have been embarrassed by the ride just as Haman was embarrassed to have taken him.

Now we see a different Haman – a Haman who is grief stricken and rushes to get home so no one can see him! He is so embarrassed that he covers his head (like we see people who have just been arrested attempting to cover who they are from the media cameras).

Let's all read the last paragraph of Chapter 6! There is a part here that is rather confusing "Since Mordecai before whom your downfall has started is of Jewish origin, you cannot stand against him – you will surely come to ruin." This was included in your homework questions! According to my research, Persians were well aware of the power of the Israelite nation's GOD. Haman, being an Agag would have grown up also aware of the fact that God himself had commanded the Israelites to totally annihilate the Amalekites. Thus when the Jew had been honored, his family felt like the God of the Jews was troubled and this would be Haman's downfall just like it had been his ancestors. You may have a better view and that's wonderful!

The discussion was cut short as the king's eunuchs arrived to quickly get Haman to attend the Queen's banquet. It was customary there for guests to be escorted to banquets.

Chapter 7 is just God putting the icing on HIS cake. You must understand the nature of God! He creates a plan for us but He will never make us do it. The obedience is up to us! We will see in this chapter of Esther's total obedience. You will see God's handprint on this entire evening. I am sure she did not sleep much last night either. So we have the king who couldn't sleep, (book, chapter, verse), we have Haman who either did not sleep working on his plan to kill Mordecai or he slept little as we know he was the first one in the king's court the next day, (book, chapter, verse) and Esther who will be making her petition to the king on behalf of the lives of not only herself but also her people. That's quite a lot on one's plate! I couldn't help but wonder if the palace was buzzing with the news about Mordecai being honored and if Esther knew or whether she and her servants had been so busy with the banquet they didn't know. I do know she would have been as thrilled as if it had been she who was honored.

We have our threesome – each with his/her own agenda at the second banquet. Does this remind you of another supper? Many commentaries call this chapter "Haman's Last Supper" and thus I thought of another 'last supper" – our Lord's. Are there any similarities? I looked at it this way. At the Lord's last supper there were also 3 agendas. The eleven disciples do not seem to have a clue as to what's going on. Their hearts are troubled. They are concerned and perplexed. They are full of questions. They are ignorant and unknowing. Does this also describe one of our 3 attendees at Haman's Last Supper? I think of King Xerxes! He doesn't have a clue as to what Esther's petition will be. He doesn't understand the pending death and doom. Then there's Jesus, our Lord, their master, the perfect Son of man, indwelt by the Father, filled with the

Spirit, aware of everything, fully attuned to the danger of the hour and moving to avert the world's greatest disaster. I think of Esther. Esther knows what's going on. She knows the evil Haman and his plot to kill the Jewish nation. Then there is Judas, the traitor, intent only on fulfilling his own desires and wants. He is totally unconcerned for the terrible results that will follow this deed because he is intent only upon the fulfillment of his own desires, his own will. Isn't that our Haman? He only wants to fulfill his own desires, his one evil want, and is unconcerned for the terrible results that will follow. Both suppers end with a man hanging upon a tree, nailed, skewered to a gallows. Now you're thinking but it wasn't Judas it was Jesus – doesn't scripture tell us that Judas went out and hanged himself just as in Esther, Haman, for all practical purposes, hangs himself. Wherever there's a cross in scripture it is always to put an evil man to death. That is what the cross of Jesus was. It was an instrument on which an evil man met death! Now for a striking difference: Check 2 Corinthians 5:21 – HE WHO KNEW NO SIN WAS MADE SIN FOR US. On the cross, Jesus became as evil as Haman for us! Esther was able through the help of God's direction to avert her disaster; Jesus knew He could have but chose not to.

Now back with our three to Haman's Last Supper. They have eaten and the king's enjoying some wine with his queen by his side when he again asked her request – "Queen Esther, what is your petition? It will be given you. What is your request? Even up to half the kingdom, it will be granted." (Do you think he's thinking a new diamond ring? More servants? A bigger kitchen?) Haman's probably still so upset over having to honor Mordecai rather than hanging him like he planned that he could care less! Soon I think the evening's conversation will interest him like no other conversation he's ever heard.

Queen Esther has been trained in the protocol of the palace for years now. Protocol is not just a modern day system of etiquette for the White House; it is almost as old as time itself. One never just blurted out something to the king ---<u>There first had to be honor shown.</u>

She begins this most critical plea with "if I have found favor with you, O king, and if it pleases your majesty, grant me my life – this is my petition. (The king, still totally in darkness is probably thinking, I lowered the scepter!) but she continues "For I and my people have been sold for destruction and slaughter and annihilation." The king is truly puzzled here – can you believe he still has no clue that Esther, his queen, is Jewish? But Esther continues, "If we had merely been sold as male and female slaves, I would have kept quiet, because no such distress would justify disturbing the king." God had worked on this eloquent speech a long time within Esther's mind.

Then the king, who reacts quickly either with anger or enjoyment, demands "Who is he? Where is the man who has dared to do such a thing?" I can just see the confused look on Haman's face wondering who had sold out the queen and her people and then the lightning bolt of understanding hits him and the blood drains from his face. Who is the enemy? It is I! I'm sure by now he's sweating profusely, his hands are beginning to quiver and his stomach has moved to his throat.

Esther quickly replies, "The adversary and enemy is this vile Haman." Vile, I love it. Even today the term means morally base, depraved, repulsive, obnoxious, disgusting, low in station, of small value. Yes, that's our Haman! Now Haman is terrified – he has to be feeling the same enormous pit in his stomach the Jewish people had been feeling – death is imminent! He will reap what he has sown! Just like us!

The king is in total disbelief. His 2nd in command, the man he trusted above all over men, had plotted to kill his queen. He jumps up in a rage and walks out of the room – he needs time to think, he needs air! He may be totally outraged but he also knows that Haman is 2nd in command of his kingdom and that he put him there. Whatever he would do to Haman for such a hideous crime would create ramifications all over the kingdom but then so did the exile of Queen Vashti (also a 2nd in command?)

Haman knew his fate! He had tricked the king into getting rid of Mordecai and throwing in all his people as a plus not knowing of the Queen's involvement. He knew his life was, shall we say, hanging on a pole! He does the first thing he can think of and starts pleading with Esther for his life. I love the next line. "Just as the king returned from the palace garden to the banquet hall, Haman was falling on the couch where Esther was reclining – is that not the neatest God thing! Just a little trip over your own feet which should have been sticking out of his mouth! This reminds me of

Potiphar's wife holding on to Joseph's jacket to accuse him unjustly. Here Haman falls quicker than the devil out of heaven giving the appearance he is molesting the queen. That was like the exclamation point on the entire evening. Haman had fallen from power!

No sooner had the king condemned Haman for molesting his wife than a covering was placed over Haman's head. Persians were not allowed to even look on the face of a condemned person and thus the condemned person's head was always covered. Then one of the eunuchs who had accompanied the king back into the room informed the king of the gallows Haman had ordered built. I found it interesting that the eunuch knew Haman had built the gallows to hang Mordecai on. I loved it when he said Mordecai was the man who spoke up to help the king. Although we're not told the details, we do know Haman is hanged on his own gallows high enough for all of Susa to see and we know that once Haman was impaled the king's fury subsided.

Now, for another fact to ponder: How is King Xerxes at last delivered from the powerful influence of someone he thought he could trust when it had been an evil influence at the time? He is delivered just like us. There has to be a revelation of evil, of sin. This we see in our story in Esther's petition. But we all have to go through this process in order for the influence of sin in our lives to be renounced! Thus we have to sentence them to death! That's what happened to Haman. His evil influence had to be erased – killed – impaled! But in order for us to get to this same place, we have to hang our sins on a cross! There are so many lessons women today can learn from the past if we'd only apply them to our lives! Please study Chapter 8 of Esther.

Now we can witness the sovereign hand of God looking out for his servants, Esther and Mordecai! Is it not poetic justice that they are finally together again! Verse one opens with King Xerxes giving Esther the estate of Haman which we know is sizable. We witness Mordecai being introduced to the king as the guardian who had raised his beloved Queen. Verse 2 illustrates the king's transferring of his signet ring (removed from Haman) to Mordecai, making him 2nd in command and to add the plump ripe cherry to the top of the sundae, Esther appointed Mordecai to run Haman's estate. BUT we still have one lingering problem! The Jews are still condemned to die. A Persian law cannot be waived even by the king himself.

Esther once again finds herself pleading with the king to overrule his edict. He can't overrule it; BUT he needs to save his Queen and her family so he comes up with the idea for Mordecai to create his own decree on behalf of the Jews that will be sealed with the king's signet ring making this edict a means of leveling the playing field! King Xerxes does have wisdom and does shine at times.

In Verse 9 we see the royal secretaries summoned on the 23rd day of the third month and wrote out all of Mordecai's orders to the Jews, and to all the government officials in the 127 provinces. This means that 3 months have passed since the casting of lots and the Jews have 9 months to prepare for battle.

Verse 11 says this edict granted the Jews in every city the right to assemble and protect themselves; to destroy, kill and annihilate any armed force of any nationality or providence that might attack them and their women and children; and to plunder the property of the enemies on the 13th day of the 12th month.

Finally, in verses 15-17 we see Mordecai dressed in royal splendor and being honored with a joyous celebration but the best news of all is found in the last verse of the chapter. "And many people of other nationalities became Jews because fear of the Jews had seized them." Would that be called 'fox hole religion' today?

I can't help but ask, if we picture our human soul with its power of will and choice but also its blindness and ignorance of the true nature of events in our lives, could we have a King Xerxes within us? Is there a Haman within us? Or is there an Esther?

In our last session, Chapter 9, and the 3rd verse of the last chapter will be studied. This will be done briefly so that I can share with you the most important lessons I have learned from the book of Esther. I'd love for each of you prior to the last session to think on this question and if time permits, write down your answer. What did the book of Esther teach you? If it taught you more than one thing, list them in the order of importance. This is what our study is all about. You, me, and our living to glorify Him! I pray you elect to serve Him even "if I perish, I perish."

Lesson Five Homework

Read the Book of Esther one more time.

1. Describe the reasons for Haman's downfall. Number them 1-3 in importance with #1 being the most important:

_____

_____

_____

_____

_____

_____

_____

_____

_____

_____

_____

2. Describe King Xerxes comparing how you felt about him when first introduced as the king who would command a queen to flaunt herself before a drunken party to the king who wisely gives Mordecai and Esther a way around his first decree.

_____

_____

_____

_____

_____

_____

_____

_____

_____

_____

_____

3. How does your Bible describe the gallows
   Haman had built?

_____

_____

_____

_____

_____

_____

_____

_____

_____

_____

_____

_____

_____

_____

4. Why do you think Queen Esther postponed asking King Xerxes her request at the first banquet?

_____

_____

_____

_____

_____

_____

_____

_____

_____

_____

_____

_____

5. How do you think the fact that Esther was a Jew was hidden until the 2nd banquet? Take into consideration that Mordecai had been inquiring about her for the past 5 years! She became queen in 479 and we're now in 474BC. Did the other Jews honor this secret ~ this mystery?

_____

_____

_____

_____

_____

_____

_____

_____

_____

_____

_____

6. All of my commentaries said that there was not a satrap (governmental official), governor or noble who fought against the Jews. Why? Was not Mordecai now 2nd in command?

_____

_____

_____

_____

_____

_____

_____

_____

_____

_____

_____

_____

_____

Now, for the nuts and bolts of our study...

7. What did the book of Esther teach you? If it taught you more than one thing, like it did me, list your lessons ending with the most important one! This is what our study is all about -- You, me, and our living to glorify Him! I have not asked this of you before, but if you can would you provide me with this list. Your name does not have to be on it, but I'd love to read how God is working within each of you. Thank you and "for such a time as this" I pray you elect to serve Him even "if I perish, I perish."

_____

_____

_____

_____

_____

_____

_____

WEEK
Six

READ CHAPTERS
8, 9, AND 10

IN CHAPTER 8, VERSE 9 IT IS STATED that "At once..." The royal secretaries were summoned (23rd day of the 3rd month) so we know that Mordecai acted quickly to relieve the fear of the Jews with this new decree. Now when we jump to Chapter 9 we see that we're at Day 13 of the twelfth month! This chapter opens with the Jews prepared to do battle with their enemies but where are they? Verse 2 says the Jews assembled to attack those seeking their destruction. No one could stand against them because they feared them. I loved verse 3, "And all the nobles of the provinces, the satraps, the governors, and the king's administrators helped the Jews because fear of Mordecai had seized them." Why was Mordecai – all of a sudden – feared? He had been 2nd in command for how long? 9 months? Scripture says …he became more and more powerful. Amen! The rest of the chapter tears at my heart.

While I was studying of the death of 500 plus 75000, I overheard an interview on TV with Jerry Falwell. The question was asked, "Where do you see the United States in the end times; what part will we play?" Falwell answered, "I don't see any reference to a nation like ours, thus, I have to assume we're no longer an important entity." That statement sent cold chills up and down my spine. Makes you wonder what caused our downfall in his mind. The next few verses portray what happened with 500 men – we're not told how many women and children – remember the edict said all were to be killed and we see that Haman's 10 sons are included in the death toll. The next few verses truly puzzle me, although I have no doubt at all that God nudged Esther to request this. She asked for one more day of killing in Susa – we're not told why – must have had a feeling that all enemies were not gone. Then the strangest request yet, and I feel this one was God given also, Esther asked for Haman's dead sons to be hanged. In Deut. 21:23 we read, "…anyone who is hung on a tree is under God's curse." Was this to be a sign from God to the people of Persia of Haman's evil? Of the evil of those who fought against the Jews? The sons had to have fought or they would not have been killed. Interesting here that the King is inquiring of Esther after the deaths of that day, what now is your request? She did not have to appeal to him. She asked for a 2nd day and he granted it. So we see that on the 2nd day of battle 300 more men were slain in Susa. The Jews however refused to take the plunder. We wonder if the women and children were harmed or if their houses, etc. were left alone? While the Jews in Susa were fighting the 2nd day, what were the Jews in the surrounding regions doing? Celebrating and resting – made it a day of feasting and joy. The Jews in Susa did the same on the 15th day so Mordecai, being a fair man, makes this occurrence a Jewish holiday of 2 days, the 14th and 15th day of the 12th month. It is still celebrated today. Why? 1.) Jews got relief from their enemies, 2.) month of sorrow turned to joy, 3.) and mourning turned to celebration. When we win our battle over sin we have the same 3 reasons to celebrate. How did they celebrate? Joyful feasting, giving of gifts of food to one another and gifts to the poor. These days were to be remembered and observed in every generation by every family, and in every province and in every city.….. should never cease to be celebrated…nor should the memory of them die out among their descendants.

Chapter 10 basically honors Mordecai…because he worked for the good of his people and spoke up for the welfare of all the Jews.

CONCLUSION

THANK YOU FOR STUDYING THE BOOK of Esther with me. She's still the beauty queen of the Bible. There are many unanswered questions, but I will never cease to believe that God never goes against His Word! Just as I so desire that you will write down your thoughts on the book of Esther, as I have done. There is one last issue that I wish to share. I truly feel God has lain this point on my heart!

One of the lessons I learned is that looking for God's absence in one's life is as important as looking for His presence. Esther was young just as we may be immature in our faith and could not help but think her God had left her at the front door of a Persian King's harem. She knew she would never leave there. Have you in your faith consciously been so intense in climbing (growing) in your faith when life around you pushes you back down to the foot of the mountain? We had Esther becoming a woman in the Jewish nation and dreaming of the day when Mordechai would select her husband. Then the soldiers entered and her bubble burst. She thought as we're so guilty of thinking that our God has left us. Just as we react this way thinking God has left us should I not be thinking – what lesson are you teaching me, God? Instead of a pity party I should be thanking God for a lesson that if learned leads me to the King. Isn't that what happened to Esther? God was there all the time.

Secondly, I learned that as a parent it may seem at times that godly parenting fails. My husband used to say when we were raising our 5 and at such different ages (6 years between our first 2 boys and our daughter and then 6 years between her and our son and daughter) that all we can do is teach them, plant the seeds of faith, and put their safety into His hands. Even when their spiritual pendulum doesn't swing the way we want it to, he would say it will swing back usually in a time of crisis or when they have children of their own, but it will swing back. Mordecai, I believe, understood what our New Testament scripture states when we are told to pray without ceasing. I can just picture him praying constantly for Esther! I believe Esther continued to pray at least twice daily facing East. Loneliness is a strange world! At her young age this would either have brought her closer to God or to the heathen idols. She could have had quite a pity party until she was selected Queen, her crisis period, and turned back to God. That's why when she requested fasting prior to approaching the king AND said her maids would join her I knew she had not forgotten the one and only Yahweh! I love that we had book, chapter and verse for that request! What a lesson for parents! All of Mordecai's teaching and witnessing of his faith to Esther had paid off! I just don't believe Esther would have her maids pray and fast to an unknown God. She would have known that to be hypocrisy. She needed serious prayer warriors. They prayed and fasted with her and for her! A request like that from a child facing a life-threatening situation would absolutely thrill my very soul!

So, parents don't' give up! Grandparents don't give up. Be a Mordecai and pray without ceasing. Lifestyle evangelism is hard to beat, and I think there was a revival going on in that palace!

Thirdly, Esther's God given beauty opened the way for the salvation of the Jewish nation. Our gift may not be physical beauty, but He has given each of us a gift or gifts and He expects us to use them to further His plan and purpose. Probably I have spent more hours in prayer over this issue than any other. What exactly did God create me to become? I'm 80 and still wondering what He wants me to be when I grow up! But daily I know He nudges me; He prepares me so that I can be ready. Esther had not been in just a 12-month preparation but a lifetime preparation. So are we!

Now for my last but most important lesson – A lesson learned that has seared my soul. I'll need your help to make my point.

Please read this list of scriptures (Select one lady to read each)

Esther 1:19
Esther 3:9
Esther 5:4 and 5:8
Esther 7:3
Esther 8:5
Esther 9:13

IF IT PLEASES THE KING! Most studies on Esther are entitled, "For such a time as this." I do think that's a thought all of us should ponder perhaps for a full day, a week, or a month of quiet time with him – time I call savoring the Savior! But if each of us lived our lives thinking daily – sometimes minute by minute – before we think we speak, "ONLY if it pleases the King will I do it, will I say it, will I think it, etc." What a difference our lives would make! That's my whole summation for each of you. Ladies think on Esther, a woman who truly lived a life pleasing to the King! First, she honored Mordecai as her substitute parent, then Hegai as her instructor; then her husband the king, and always THE eternal KING. We should strive to do no less.

I taught this study to our ladies; we enjoyed having the King Xerxes banquet; and at the end I presented each a beaded bracelet to wear stating, "If it pleases the King" as a reminder of how we should live our lives from this day on. Go and do likewise!

For those of you who wondered what eventually happened to Esther – did they live happily ever after? There are lots of stories.

The one that seems most agreed upon is that she and King Xerxes were slain in the palace at Susa as Artaxerxes (remember the heir) plotted the king's overthrow. Most stories said Artaxerxes had been raised by Vashti to take over the throne which was rightfully his. Many scholars believe Vashti was really Amestris, the mother of Artaxerxes, born in 483 BC (time of the king's banquets when Vashti refused to appear in public). We do know Artaxerxes ruled from 464 – 425 BC (would have made him 19 years old when his reign began). Artaxerxes ruled during the times of Ezra and Nehemiah (Nehemiah 2:1; 5:14; 13:6). History also records that "Amestris" exercised great power as the queen mother. So, if all that is true our Esther ruled as a God-centered woman and died as a Queen never having any children!

Author's Note:
Additions to the book of Esther as found in the Bible were researched by the Author.

THE PERSIAN DINNER RECIPIES

Persian food is a wonderful combination of exotic flavors and easy preparation. You'll find the flavors are cool and mild with sweet hints of fruit and pleasant herbs. This menu will serve eight. If you wish, you may halve the recipes to create a romantic dinner for two.

To recreate the mood of Esther's feast for Xerxes, be sure to have plenty of candles burning. Sprinkle a few rose petals across the table if you like. For fun, set the feast on a low table and invite your guests to recline comfortably on cushions as they eat.

Platters of fresh fruit are served as an appetizer.

Cucumber Dill Dip
Means to be eaten with flat bread

1 (32 oz.) container of plain yogurt
3 cucumbers, peeled and diced into small pieces
1 clove garlic, minced
2 shallots, finely chopped
1 tsp. salt
1 tsp. pepper

Directions: Stir together in a medium bowl. Best to make night before.

Flatbread

If your grocer does not carry flatbread, simply purchase whole grain pitas, and cut each into four triangles by cutting down the middle in an "x" pattern.

Place pieces on a cookie sheet and roast at 250 degrees for 10 minutes until firm. Do not allow these to brown or they will dry out.

You can give them a quick drizzle of olive oil and sprinkle with garlic or onion powder before roasting if you would like a bolder flavor. One of our ladies used cheese and it was quite good.

Herbed Feasting Rice

This rice is a delicious accompaniment for chicken or beef. Use fresh herbs if you can. This rice may be added in the day before and reheated before serving.

4 cups uncooked long-grain white rice (may substitue jasmine rice)
3 Tbs. vegetable oil
1 bunch fresh dill, chopped
½ cup fresh parsley, chopped
½ cup fresh cilantro, chopped
2 cups fava beans (may omit if your grocer doesn't carry them)
1 tsp. ground tumeric
1 tsp. ground cinnamon
1 tsp. salt
1 tsp. pepper

Cont.

Directions: Cook rice according to package directions. Stir in all remaining ingredients. Cover and simmer on lowest heat for 5-10 minutes or until well heated. If you have crispy rice on the bottom of the pan, this is considered a delicacy, and served to the most favored guest.

Chicken in Pomegranate Sauce

This makes a beautiful presentation right from the pan. Pomegranate molasses can be ordered from your grocer.

> 2 Tbs. Olive oil
> 1 onion, chopped
> 4 skinless, boneless chicken breast halves, each cut in half lengthwise
> 1 cup fine ground walnuts (save some whole to use as a garnish)
> 1 (10 fluid ounce) bottle of pomegranate molasses

Directions: Heat olive oil in a large skillet over medium high heat. Add onions and stir-fry until soft and transparent, then remove from the skillet. Add chicken breasts, several at a time, and brown them on each side. Set them aside until all have been browned. This will not cook the chicken thoroughly but will seal in the juices before you cook the chicken again. Place the ground walnuts in the skillet. Turn heat down to medium and cook for 5 minutes or until they are a rich brown color. Place chicken and onions over walnuts in the skillet. Over this pour in the pomegranate molasses. Turn heat down to low and cover the skillet. Cook for 20 minutes, stirring every 5 minutes or so, until chicken is cooked through. Before serving, arrange chicken in a starburst in the pan, and sprinkle a few whole walnuts in the middle and along the sides.

Roasted Lamb Kabob with Mint

Kabobs can be made with beef or pork.

Kabobs:

> 2 lbs. Lamb, pork, or beef cut in large cubes
> 1 package cherry tomatoes
> 1 onion – quartered
> 1 green pepper, cut in thick wedges

Marinade:

> 1 (8 oz.) container of plain low-fat yogurt
> 1 onion finely chopped
> 1 tsp. dried mint flakes (available in the spice rack) do not use mint extract.

Directions: Create kabobs, alternating meat with vegetables. Combine all marinade ingredients and spoon over each kabob. Marinate 6 hours or overnight. Heat grill to high, then return to medium-high heat. Grill each kabob, turning as needed, until the center cut of meat is grilled to desired degree.

TIME LINE FOR BOOK OF ESTHER

486 BC

King Xerxes I began his reign
Married Queen Vashti
Allowed Jews who had been exiled there to return home
if they so desired

483 BC

Book of Esther begins
180 days feast is in full swing to persuade his princes,
nobles, etc. to follow him into battle to conquer Greece
Queen Vashti exiled
Artaxerxes, heir to the throne, born to Queen Vashti

480 BC

King Xerxes won a great battle at Thermopylae BUT
Was defeated at a battle at Salamis where he watched
1/2 – 1/3 of his Navy destroyed. He returned home
defeated and depressed.

479 BC

Selection of new queen begins
Esther crowned queen

474 BC

Haman's plot; Mordecai honored; Esther goes before
King uninvited; Haman killed; enemies of Jews defeated

465 BC

According to A.S. Van Der Woude's, "The World of the Bible",
Vol. 1, King Xerxes and his family were assassinated in their own
bedchambers by Artabanus, and Xerxes is succeeded by his son,
Artaxerxes. Plot supposedly led by exiled Queen Vashti and
her son.

*103 years after Nebuchadnezzar had taken the Jews into captivity (II Kings 25); 54
years after Jerubbabel led the first group of Jewish exiles back to Jerusalem; 25 years
before Ezra led the second group. Babylon fell in 539 BC; 56 years prior to Xerxes' rule.

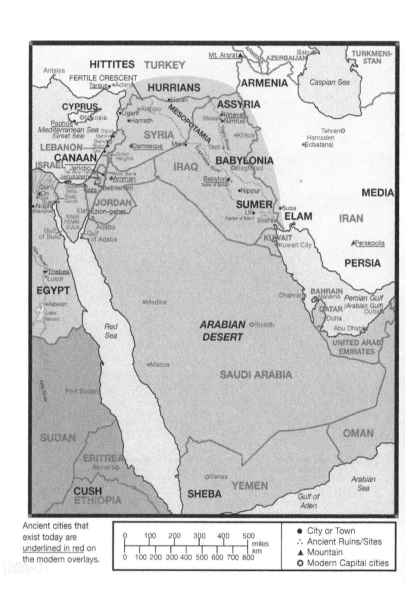

Ancient cities that exist today are <u>underlined in red</u> on the modern overlays.

0 100 200 300 400 500 miles	● City or Town
0 100 200 300 400 500 600 700 800 km	∴ Ancient Ruins/Sites
	▲ Mountain
	✪ Modern Capital cities

Author's Note

ALICE K. RAWLINGS IS AN EXPERIENCED
Bible teacher and speaker. Her goal in life has been
to equip ladies to be Christ-centered and vocal about
it! She serves as the Women's Bible Study teacher at
Christ's Community Church where her husband, Scott,
has ministered for the past 50 years! They are the parents of 5 adult children – one, now the teaching pastor
and one grandson the youth minister at CCC. Besides
their ministry at CCC they are very active in Uganda

having built a baby rescue mission, and help fund two orphanages. Two adult orphans have lived with them for the past 6 years graduating from a Bible College and now earning their master's degree to return home to teach and preach.

To my husband, Scott Rawlings:

Thank you for your patience with my sleepless nights and my addiction to Queen Esther!